MCO P5354.1D
MPE
14 Apr 03

MARINE CORPS ORDER P5354.1D W/CH 1

From: Commandant of the Marine Corps
To: Distribution List

Subj: MARINE CORPS EQUAL OPPORTUNITY (EO) MANUAL (SHORT TITLE: EOM)

Ref: (a) DoDDir 1350.2
       (b) SECNAVINST 5350.14
       (c) SECNAVINST 5354.1

Encl: (1) LOCATOR SHEET

Report Required: Annual Equal Opportunity Data Summary (Report
                  Control Symbol MC-5354-01), par. 3002.5

1. <u>Purpose</u>. To publish the EO policies, procedures, responsibilities, and
standards by which all personnel will be treated while in the service of the
United States Marine Corps, and implement the provisions of the references.

2. <u>Cancellation</u>. MCO P5354.1C.

3. <u>Summary of Revision</u>. This revision includes major chapter and paragraph
modifications, establishes new EO complaint reporting timelines and training
requirements, clarifies reporting procedures, and identifies survey
requirements. Because of the substantial number of changes and new
procedures, this Manual should be reviewed in its entirety.

4. <u>Recommendations</u>. Recommend changes to this Manual are encouraged and
should be submitted to Commandant of the Marine Corps (MPE), via the
appropriate chain of command.

5. <u>Reserve Applicability</u>. This Manual is applicable to the Marine Corps
Reserve.

6. <u>Clarification</u>. Reviewed and approved this date.

S. T. JOHNSON
By direction

DISTRIBUTION: PCN 10207973900

        Copy to: 7000027 (20)
                  7000110 (5)
                  8145004, 005 (2)
                  7000144/7000093, 8145001 (1)

DISTRIBUTION STATEMENT A: Approved for public release; distribution is unlimited

DEPARTMENT OF THE NAVY
HEADQUARTERS UNITED STATES MARINE CORPS
2 NAVY ANNEX
WASHINGTON, DC 20380-1775

MCO P5354.1D Ch1
MPE
28 AUG 2006

MARINE CORPS ORDER P5354.1D Ch1

From: Commandant of the Marine Corps
To: Distribution List

Subj: MARINE CORPS EQUAL OPPORTUNITY (EO) MANUAL (SHORT TITLE: EOM)

Encl: (1) New page inserts to MCO P5354.1D

1. Purpose. To transmit new pages to MCO P5354.1D.

2. Action. Remove pages 3-3, 3-4, 3-5, and 3-6 of the basic order and replace with 3-3, 3-4, 3-5, and 3-6 of the enclosure.

M. L. RHODES
Deputy Commandant for
Manpower and Reserve Affairs
Acting

DISTRIBUTION: PCN 1027973901

    Copy to: 7000027 (20)
             7000110 (5)
             8145004, 005 (2)
             7000144/7000093, 8145001 (1)

LOCATOR SHEET

Subj: MARINE CORPS EQUAL OPPORTUNITY MANUAL (SHORT TITLE: EOM)

Location: _____

(Indicates the location(s) of the copy(ies) of this Manual.)

RECORD OF CHANGES

Log completed change action as indicated.

Change Number	Date of Change	Date Entered	Signature of Person Incorporated Change

CONTENTS

INTRODUCTION

0001. <u>PURPOSE</u>. To incorporate equal opportunity (EO) into the Marine Corps' ethos and leadership philosophy.

0002. <u>APPLICABILITY</u>. The provisions of this Manual apply to Marines and other Armed Forces personnel assigned to, or serving with, Marine Corps units, and civilian supervisors of military personnel. The policies and provisions of the Equal Employment Opportunity (EEO) Program concerning civilian personnel employed by the Marine Corps are provided in separate Department of the Navy (DON) EEO regulations and are not covered in this Manual.

0003. <u>POLICY</u>. The Marine Corps will provide EO for all military members without regard to age, color, gender, race, religion, or national origin, consistent with the law, regulations, and the requirements for physical and mental abilities.

0004. <u>DEFINITION OF TERMS</u>. To ensure uniform understanding of the terms that have special significance/meaning relative to the Marine Corps EO policies and procedures, definitions are provided in Appendix F. Terms that have special meaning relative to specific chapters of this Manual are defined in those chapters.

0005. <u>ADDITIONAL REFERENCES</u>. In addition to the guidance provided in this Manual, a listing of pertinent references is at Appendix G.

CHAPTER 1

PURPOSE AND OBJECTIVES

CHAPTER 1

PURPOSE AND OBJECTIVES

1000. SCOPE

1. The Marine Corps is built on the trust and teamwork shared between
individual Marines and their leaders. Inherent in this trust is the
understanding that fair, scrupulous, and unbiased treatment is the Marine
Corps leadership standard. In keeping with this leadership philosophy, this
Manual will be applied in every command policy, action, and program.

2. The responsibility for accomplishing equal opportunity is not dependent
on authority or solely the function of any special staff officer. Rather,
all Marines are expected to promote camaraderie among individuals, regardless
of age, color, gender, race, religion, or national origin, by setting an
example of unprejudiced actions and identifying unfair practices to higher
authority via the chain of command.

1001. PURPOSE. Unlawful discriminatory practices within the Marine Corps
are counterproductive and unacceptable. Discrimination undermines morale,
reduces combat readiness, and prevents maximum utilization and development of
the Marine Corps' most vital asset, its "people". The policy of the Marine
Corps is to provide equality of treatment and the opportunity for all Marines
to achieve their full potential based solely upon individual merit, fitness,
and ability.

1002. OBJECTIVES. The primary objective is to integrate equal opportunity
into every aspect of Marine Corps life. Specific objectives are as follows:

1. To build and maintain a cohesive combat ready corps of Marines who are
focused and determined to accomplish their mission.

2. To promote teamwork and cohesion through the elimination of prejudice and
harassment.

3. To ensure equal opportunity exists for all Marines.

    a. We must ensure that every Marine is prized and appreciated for their
individual worth, and that each Marine is afforded full opportunity for
professional achievement.

    b. The obligation of each member of the chain of command is to ensure
that this sense of fairness is constant and genuine. An environment of
fairness for all Marines is crucial to building a warfighting team.

CHAPTER 2

UNIT EO CLIMATE

CHAPTER 2

UNIT EO CLIMATE

2000. GENERAL

1. The organizational climate of a unit is the responsibility of the commander. Sound leadership is the key to eliminating all forms of unlawful discrimination, and those in supervisory positions must foster an environment free of inappropriate behavior. All individuals in the unit must be treated fairly and with mutual respect.

2. Unit personnel should be allowed and encouraged to address situations that detract from the unit's cohesion and its ability to perform the mission. Commanders must ensure that the Informal Resolution System described in paragraph 5002.1 and the Request Mast process can be used by all without intimidation and/or fear of reprisal.

3. The motto on the Great Seal of the United States reads, "E Pluribus Unum," Out of Many, One. Just as our one Nation was formed from many people, a commander must form one cohesive unit from many individuals. To accomplish this, command involvement in the areas addressed in the following paragraphs is necessary.

2001. CHAIN OF COMMAND. The chain of command is the primary and preferred channel for correcting discriminatory practices and for communicating EO matters. The chain of command is the succession of commanding officers from a superior to a subordinate through which command is exercised.

1. Individuals who believe they have been subjected to discrimination or inappropriate behavior should report the incident to the chain of command if they believe they are unable to resolve the problem by themselves or the incident is criminal in nature. MCO 1700.23 (Request Mast) provides chain of command clarification for EO complaints filed through Request Mast procedures.

2. EO is everyone's responsibility. Anyone who witnesses an act of discrimination has a responsibility to address, correct or report the inappropriate behavior immediately. Other specific responsibilities are identified in chapter 3 of this Manual.

2002. MONITORING OF COMMAND CLIMATE

1. Symptoms of a breakdown in unit cohesion may appear in new and varied forms. Proactive measures must be taken to prevent possible erosion of the command's readiness posture. This can best be accomplished through concerned leadership and open, responsive channels of communication.

2. To identify areas requiring command attention, the commander must monitor all incidents that would reflect discord among Marines. The analysis of such data, in conjunction with other management tools, is invaluable to the commander in assessing the cohesion of the command.

3. The following is a list of possible indicators of unit unrest or turmoil.
Although not all inclusive, these indicators have proven to be reliable in
the past:

    a. Increase in racial, ethnic or sexual harassment complaints/incidents
among Service members, their family members, and civilian employees.

    b. Incidents with racial/ethnic/sexual overtones that may occur on base
or in the surrounding civilian community.

    c. Appearance of racist, religiously intolerant, or prejudicial
literature, signs, graffiti, etc.

    d. Marines wearing civilian clothing or tattoos with organizational
insignia or words that are racist/sexist or gang-related.

    e. De facto or group-imposed segregation in command billeting, mess
halls, clubs, and recreation areas.

4. If used and conducted appropriately, command assessments are valuable
tools in determining command climate. Commanders are required to assess
their command EO climate within 90 days of assumption of command, and ensure
proactive strategies are initiated to monitor unit progress if needed.
Although either the Military Equal Opportunity Climate Survey (MEOCS) or the
Marine Corps Command Assessment Survey (Windows) (MCCASWin) may be used to
meet this requirement, the MEOCS is the preferred survey. Detailed
information on both of these surveys can be provided by the local Equal
Opportunity Advisor (EOA). Commands that have been assessed within 90 days
of a new commander's arrival are not required to be reassessed.

    a. MEOCS. MEOCS was designed by the Defense Equal Opportunity
Management Institute (DEOMI) to assess the EO climate of a unit. The MEOCS
may be requested from the DEOMI, utilizing the format and instructions
provided in Appendix L. Since only the requesting commander will see the
results of the survey, this is a good tool for commanders to assess the EO
climate in their units and take corrective actions where necessary. The
results also give the commander an overall comparison of other Marine Corps
units that have taken the survey. Data collected by the MEOCS is used to get
an overall picture of the Marine Corps.

    b. MCCASWin. This system is a computer generated survey that measures
perceptions and attitudes of command members on discrimination and
organizational factors such as assignments, training, leadership,
communications, interpersonal relations, complaints, discipline, performance
evaluation, promotions, and general issues. The MCCASWin is an abbreviated
version of the Marine Corps Climate Survey (MCCS). The MCCS is administered
periodically to a random sampling of the entire Marine Corps and Marine Corps
Reserve. The MCCASWin results can represent an EO climate snapshot for the
commander. It is available at the commander's request and administered by
the EOA. The EOA will brief the commanding officer on the survey results.

5. Rapid command response to EO issues must be visible to all members of the
unit. The absence of a visible response can result in increased apprehension
and polarization. No incident having an effect on EO can be overlooked or
discounted, regardless of how insignificant or limited its involvement may
appear on the surface. Every incident should be addressed and if necessary
recorded and reported through the chain of command for resolution.

2003. <u>MAINTENANCE OF STATISTICAL DATA</u>

1. The maintenance and frequent review of statistical data relating to personnel can alert commanders to the development of trends and patterns that may affect the command's EO climate.

2. Appendix A is an ideal tool to manage the EO environment. The Marine Corps Total Force System (MCTFS) may be of assistance in compiling the majority of the data shown in Appendix A. The statistical data compiled is not reported to CMC; however, EO is a functional area open to review for compliance by the Inspector General (IG). The IG Checklist at Appendix H is provided for your information and guide to ensure compliance.

3. Marine Corps Reserve Support Command is exempt from maintaining data on Individual Ready Reserve (IRR) Marines.

2004. <u>COMMUNICATION/INFORMATION, AND AWARDS PROGRAMS</u>

1. All unit personnel should be aware of the command's EO policies, available communication channels, and all relevant information discussed in this Manual. Full use should be made of leadership training, unit information programs, command newsletters, bulletin boards, formations, and welcome-aboard and indoctrination briefs to achieve this goal.

2. Effective internal information and public affairs programs provide an excellent means of demonstrating the command's commitment to EO and the resultant combat readiness. To ensure these programs support their EO objectives, commanders will:

    a. Ensure that historical/cultural events of significant interest within the command are given proper recognition in installation or local newspapers within the context of the Marine Corps' ethos. Appendix J contains a list of DoD recognized special emphasis observances.

    b. Develop and release to public and internal media, feature stories concerning efforts and commitment by the Marine Corps to ensure fair treatment of all personnel.

    c. Be alert to any journalistic practices that degrade or stereotype people based on age, color, gender, race, religion or national origin.

    d. Per the current edition of SECNAVINST 5720.44, develop and maintain sound community relations with local government leaders and civic organizations who support EO for Marines in the community (this pertains to host commanders at the base/camp/station level and above).

3. Commands are encouraged to participate in the various EO, leadership, and community service award celebrations sponsored annually by civilian organizations. For additional information on these various awards, contact CMC (MPE). Commands are highly encouraged to establish local awards to recognize those military and civilian personnel whose achievements have significantly contributed to the esprit and teamwork of the Marine Corps. In identifying those individuals who merit recognition, commanders must ensure the same standards are applied to all members of the command.

2005. CAREER DEVELOPMENT/ASSIGNMENT

1. The opportunity for advancement is essential to the morale and readiness of a command. To ensure equality of opportunity for career progression and development, commanders will ensure that unlawful discrimination is not a factor in screening processes.

2. Assignments have an impact on advancement potential. Commanders will ensure that all assignments (primary duty, work details, transfer quotas, etc.) are based on grade, occupational skill requirements, performance, and the needs of the Marine Corps. Marines will not be denied assignments for which they are qualified because of age, color, gender, race, religion, or national origin unless otherwise authorized/required by law or regulation.

2006. TRAINING

1. One of the primary means for implementing the command EO objectives is through leadership training. Reference (a) mandates that all military personnel, including general officers, receive training in EO, human relations, and prevention of sexual harassment. Specific EO training requirements are located in chapter 4 of this Manual.

2. All commands have training material available to them. Every major command has an EOA assigned who maintains a Training Information Resources (TIR) Library. The purpose of these libraries is to provide resources for commands or individuals to use in strengthening the cohesion and trust within units. The TIR Library includes videos, books, lesson plans, posters, and other materials. The EOA is responsible to maintain, update, and manage the TIR Library. Equal Opportunity Representatives (EOR) will coordinate with the nearest (geographic) EOA to use these resources to conduct training at their units.

2007. MILITARY JUSTICE. Injustice perceived by an individual Marine or group of Marines, whether real or imagined, has a detrimental effect on unit readiness and morale. Therefore, commanders will:

1. Ensure military justice and administrative separation functions in the command are performed free of discrimination.

2. Investigate all cases where discrimination is suspected or alleged to be a factor in the judicial process.

3. Monitor command disciplinary statistics for possible trends of unequal treatment.

2008. DISCRIMINATION. Discrimination is the illegal treatment of a person or group based on age, color, gender, race, religion, or national origin. Discrimination also includes persons condoning, ignoring, or failing to correct negative and hostile working environments, where one or more of the discriminatory factors mentioned above is present, during the performance of their duties. All forms of discrimination, such as racism, sexism, and religious intolerance, can occur not just through the acts of individuals, but within the systems, policies and procedures of an organization. Such unacceptable conduct, if uncorrected, will eventually poison a unit's cohesion and morale.

2009. SEXUAL HARASSMENT

1. Definition. Sexual harassment is a form of discrimination that involves unwelcome sexual advances, requests for sexual favors, and other verbal or physical conduct of a sexual nature when:

    a. Submission to such conduct is made either explicitly or implicitly a term or condition of a person's job, pay, career, or;

    b. Submission to or rejection of such conduct by a person is used as a basis for career or employment decisions affecting that person, or;

    c. Such conduct has the purpose or effect of unreasonably interfering with an individual's work performance or creates an intimidating, hostile, or offensive working environment.

2. This definition emphasizes that workplace conduct, to be actionable as "abusive work environment" harassment, need not result in concrete psychological harm to the victim, but rather need only be so severe or pervasive that a reasonable person would perceive, and the victim does perceive, the work environment as hostile or abusive. (Note: Due to the unique nature of military life, "workplace" is an expansive term and includes conduct on or off duty, 24 hours a day.)

3. Any person in a supervisory or command position who fails to correct, or uses/condones any form of sexual behavior to control, influence, or affect the career, pay, or job of a military member or civilian employee is engaging in sexual harassment. Similarly, any military member or civilian employee who makes deliberate or repeated unwelcome verbal comments, gestures, or physical contact of a sexual nature in the workplace is also engaging in sexual harassment.

4. Commanders, supervisors, managers, and all others in leadership positions will neither tolerate nor fail to correct sexual harassment by their subordinates, nor will they allow the existence of hostile work environments. Any such violations of Marine Corps policy are subject to appropriate disciplinary or administrative action, when substantiated.

5. Sexual harassment is a criminal offense punishable under the UCMJ as a violation of U.S. Navy Regulations.

6. Willfully submitting false allegations is a violation of U.S. Navy Regulations and is punishable under the UCMJ.

7. DON policy on sexual harassment, contained in SECNAVINST 5300.26 and MCO 1000.9, requires commanders to take appropriate action in each substantiated incident of sexual harassment. Appropriate action includes, but is not limited to, formal or informal counseling, non punitive letter of caution, security clearance revocation, adverse fitness report, nonjudicial punishment (NJP), or court-martial. Additionally, officers and enlisted personnel of the Navy or Marine Corps will be processed for administrative separation on the first substantiated incident of sexual harassment that involves any of the following circumstances:

    a.   Threats or attempts to influence another's career or job for sexual favors; or

    b.   Rewards in exchange for sexual favors; or

    c.   Physical contact of a sexual nature that, if charged as a violation of the UCMJ, could result in a punitive discharge.

2010. <u>RACIAL INCIDENTS</u>

1.   Whenever an incident occurs that appears to have a racial/ethnic cause, the following guidelines should be used:

    a.   An incident should be considered as a racial/ethnic incident if it involves members of two or more racial/ethnic groups where racial/ethnic factors were the precipitating cause, or during the incident, became a motivating factor.

    b.   Any incident which involves members of the command expressing or demonstrating open support for known racist organizations or groups should be considered a racial/ethnic incident.

2.   A racial/ethnic incident is defined as <u>significant</u> if it contains one or more of the following elements:

    a.   Death or personal injury that requires hospitalization of an individual.

    b.   Property damage in excess of $1,000 as the result of a racial incident.

    c.   A security/reaction force is alerted.

    d.   Racially motivated, riotous or rebellious conduct that involves defiance or overt contemptuous acts directed by a group toward military authority.

    e.   Racially motivated assaults involving use of a deadly weapon.

    f.   An incident in which a racist organization is identified or perceived as being involved.

    g.   An incident which, in the commander's opinion, may result in escalation or future incidents that may negatively affect the command's readiness.

3.   All significant incidents will be reported to CMC (POC) with an information copy to CMC (MPE) upon occurrence, per MCO 5740.2. Incidents that are not initially identified as having racial/ethnic overtones but later, through investigation, reveal racial/ethnic causes, will be reported upon that determination. Subsequent information, to comply with the requirements of MCO 5740.2, will be submitted within 30 days of the incident. The submission of the DASH Report will be in accordance with chapter 5 of this Manual.

2011. PREVENTION OF DISCRIMINATION. Methods to prevent discrimination and forms of harassment include:

1. Being proactive and ensuring that all EO complaints are thoroughly investigated. Addressing incidents of discrimination as quickly as possible. These behaviors/problems do not go away when ignored.

2. Publicizing Marine Corps and local command EO policy. Stressing leadership accountability and emphasizing teamwork. Stating that discrimination in any form is adverse to mission accomplishment and will not be tolerated in the unit.

3. Ensuring all Marines are aware of the avenues of filing EO complaints and actions that will be taken against personnel in substantiated cases. A capable, trusted method of communicating EO complaints strengthens our Corps against negative values and inappropriate behavior.

4. Setting the example by knowing what sexual harassment is and refusing to condone it. Establishing a command climate that precludes sexual harassment and is reflected at each level of the chain of command. Marines must not only refrain from sexual harassment but also actively counter and report such actions immediately. Counseling harassers when sexual harassment is viewed even if a complaint is not filed.

2012. REPORTING INAPPROPRIATE BEHAVIOR

1. Marine Corps personnel who are recipients of inappropriate, or perceived inappropriate, discriminatory behavior shall be afforded the opportunity to seek redress. The Marine Corps provides two methods for resolving EO complaints: formally and informally. The decision on which method to use rests with recipient, not with command personnel. Command personnel may make a recommendation to the recipient but in no way will they order a recipient to use a specific method to resolve complaints. Once a complaint has been forwarded to the commanding officer for action, the method of resolution is then left to the commanding officer. The complete complaint procedures are located in chapter 5 of this Manual.

2. Any person within the supervisory chain of command who receives a formal EO complaint will forward the complaint immediately to the commanding officer for action. If a Marine is involved, the command must then report the complaint to the CMC (MPE) in accordance with the procedures identified in chapter 5 of this Manual.

2013. USE OF BASE AND UNIT FACILITIES. Base and unit facilities must be responsive to the needs of the command and must support the commander's EO policy. Commanders must ensure that EO exists in the decision process regarding the use and operation of all base/unit facilities, to include barracks/living areas, exchanges, commissaries, religious activities, and entertainment/recreation facilities. All unit leaders must ensure compliance with this policy, and be alert to any instance of discrimination. Commanders will monitor the operation of all facilities to ensure that neither segregation nor discriminatory practices occur.

2014. OFF-BASE FACILITIES AND HOUSING

1. DoD's housing policy emphasizes the civilian community as the primary source of housing facilities; therefore, the elimination of discrimination against military personnel seeking off-base housing must receive continuous command attention.

2. To ensure equal opportunity in housing programs, commanders will:

    a. Ensure off-base housing and facilities are not restricted to Marine Corps personnel based on age, color, gender, race, religion, or national origin. If irregularities or complaints arise, they should be forwarded to the installation commander.

    b. Ensure that housing referral offices provide assistance to all Marines in obtaining adequate off-base housing as outlined in MCO P11000.22.

3. The installation commander is the Marine Corps' representative to the surrounding civilian community and the officer primarily responsible for fostering equal treatment for military personnel and family members in that community. Installation commanders will take the following steps to ensure equal treatment for military personnel and their family members in the local community:

    a. Establish and maintain a working relationship with community councils or civilian community leaders to address instances and/or patterns of alleged discriminatory practices, and develop recommendations toward resolving those problems.

    b. Develop and maintain procedures for liaison with appropriate local, state, and federal agencies for solving discrimination problems.

    c. Use the worldwide authority and responsibility to impose off-limits sanctions, per MCO 1620.2, should other actions prove unsuccessful. Ensure that military personnel are advised of:

        (1) The right to initiate civil suits against discriminatory establishments, appropriate officials to notify in cases of discrimination in public facilities, and proper complaint procedures.

        (2) The provisions of Titles II and III of the Civil Rights Act of 1964 and the Fair Housing Amendments Act of 1988.

    d. Ensure that legal assistance officers are knowledgeable of procedures for handling complaints concerning the applicability of the Civil Rights Act of 1964 and for requesting the Attorney General to institute civil suits.

4. The commander's EO objectives must actively promote the nondiscriminatory assignment of military family members to public schools in the community and the equal treatment of military members in civilian adult education programs.

2015. DISCRIMINATION BY PRIVATE ORGANIZATIONS

1. The DON policy prohibits Marine Corps units or Marine Corps-sponsored organizations from using the facilities of organizations having discriminatory membership policies. However, membership and participation in

such organizations or clubs by Marines as private citizens may be permitted as long as such participation is not contrary to good order and discipline. Membership in such organizations is not encouraged and should be considered in light of the impact on trust among fellow Marines.

2.   Commanders will ensure that personnel who are members of organizations or associations that have discriminatory practices that are incompatible with official Marine Corps policy avoid activities on behalf of the organizations/associations that give the appearance of Marine Corps affiliation. When, in the opinion of the commander, the undermining effect of discriminatory practices of bona fide private organizations weakens the morale of their respective commands, "off-limits" sanctions may be justified. The facts relating to the findings of discrimination and the impact that it has on the command should be developed by the local Armed Forces Disciplinary Control Board (MCO 1620.2), which allows all parties a full and fair opportunity to present their case.

3.   Marines must reject participation in organizations that espouse supremacist causes; attempt to create illegal discrimination based on race, creed, color, sex, religion, or national origin; advocate the use of force or violence; or otherwise engage in efforts to deprive individuals of their civil rights. Active participation, such as publicly demonstrating or rallying, fund raising, recruiting and training members, organizing or leading such organizations, or otherwise engaging in activities in relation to such organizations or in furtherance of the objectives of such organizations that are viewed by command to be detrimental to the good order, discipline, or mission accomplishment of the unit, is incompatible with military service, and is therefore, prohibited. Commanders have the authority to employ the full range of administrative procedures, including separation or appropriate disciplinary action, against military personnel who actively participate in such groups. Functions of command include vigilance about the existence of such activities; active use of investigative authority to include a prompt and fair complaint process; and use of administrative powers, such as counseling, reprimands, orders, and performance evaluations to deter such activities.

CHAPTER 3

RESPONSIBILITIES

CHAPTER 3

RESPONSIBILITIES

3000. GENERAL. The Commandant of the Marine Corps establishes and guides the Marine Corps EO policy. All Marines share in the responsibility to achieve a Marine Corps that is free of unlawful discrimination. The intent of the Marine Corps EO policy remains as outlined in 1972 by then Commandant Robert Cushman in a letter to all general officers and commanding officers:

> I view our human relations efforts as major steps in helping the Corps to attain that environment of equal opportunity, understanding, and professionalism so vital to our future effectiveness. That environment, when combined with an open, two-way channel of communication among all Marines, will permit us to devote our total energies toward maintaining what our Nation needs and expects from us, a combat ready Corps of Marines.

3001. MANPOWER EQUAL OPPORTUNITY BRANCH

1. The responsibility for the Marine Corps EO Program is a function of the Deputy Commandant for Manpower and Reserve Affairs. The EO Program is managed by the Manpower Plans and Policy Division (MP), and is executed by the Manpower Equal Opportunity Branch (MPE). CMC (MPE) develops and administers EO policies, programs, and activities for CMC, and serves as liaison/advisor regarding manpower issues as they relate to Equal Opportunity. CMC (MPE) shall maintain responsibility and oversight for all minority issues.

2. CMC (MPE) will publish the Commandant of the Marine Corps' Equal Opportunity Statement. New statements are published subsequent to a change of Commandant.

3. CMC (MPE) is responsible for the preparation of the annual Military Equal Opportunity Assessment (MEOA). The MEOA will be prepared in accordance with current DoD directives using information obtained from databases and information from the Equal Opportunity Data Summary Reports (MC-5354-01). The annual MEOA will be distributed to all major commands, and commanders are encouraged to use the information contained in the MEOA to develop their own EO goals and directions.

4. CMC (MPE) shall maintain and monitor the Marine Corps Discrimination and Sexual Harassment (DASH) Reporting System. The primary purpose of the system is to advise the CMC of transgressions occurring in the Corps. It is also used to provide statistical data and monitor compliance with complaint timelines.

5. CMC (MPE), in conjunction with DEOMI, will periodically provide commanders with updated statistics on EO related issues, such as sexual harassment, discrimination, and the EO climate/environment.

6. CMC (MPE) will coordinate and assume oversight of the Officer Requirements Review Board (ORRB), and will generate the findings and recommendations of the board to CMC. The membership of the ORRB consists of: Deputy Director, Manpower Plans and Policy Division (MP); Deputy Director,

Personnel Management Division (MM); Head, Reserve Affairs Plans and Policy Branch (RA); Chief of Staff, Training and Education Command (MCCDC); Commanding Officer, Officer Candidates School (OCS); Commanding Officer, The Basic School (TBS); Chief of Staff, Marine Corps Recruiting Command (MCRC); and Deputy Director, Public Affairs Division (PA). CMC (MPE) will disseminate information and coordinating instructions to participating agencies and assemble the ORRB as directed by DC M&RA. The primary purpose of the ORRB is to review current policies and procedures for recruiting, training and retaining the officer corps. In addition, it establishes baselines and reviews measures of effectiveness to determine if current policies are producing desired results. CMC (MPE) will coordinate additional requirements tasked to the ORRB as directed by DC M&RA.

3002. <u>COMMANDERS</u>

1. Commanders are responsible for establishing effective EO objectives within their command. They must ensure that EO is applied in every command policy, action, and program. They shall establish policies and procedures to ensure the periodic assessment and update of their EO objectives. EO objectives vary with the level of command.

2. All Commanders will:

    a. Be responsible for publicizing, implementing, and enforcing the Marine Corps policy on EO and discrimination.

    b. Ensure that EO complaints received by the chain of command are promptly investigated in a fair, impartial manner, and are appropriately resolved without fear of reprisal, intimidation, or retaliation. The procedures for processing complaints are located in chapter 5 of this Manual.

    c. Publish a command policy statement on EO (which includes sexual harassment) to support the EO objectives. This statement should include complaint procedures and identify the possible consequences of engaging in any form of discrimination. The policy statement should be prominently posted on all unit bulletin boards, in common areas, high traffic areas and discussed by unit commanders during leadership training.

    d. Ensure follow-ups are conducted with personnel involved in investigations to ensure consistent enforcement, timeline compliance, and that reprisal or retaliation has not occurred. Discrimination and sexual harassment issues should be made a special interest item in the command's inspection program.

3. <u>Force Commanders, Commanding Generals and Regimental/Group Commanders</u>. If an EOA is not assigned to the command, the Commanding General or Commanding Officer will designate an officer or SNCO for collateral duty as the Command Equal Opportunity Manager (CEOM) to manage the EO objectives for their command. The CEOM does not function as the command EOA but only as the EO program manager; all EOA requirements shall be directed to the nearest EOA. A letter of agreement shall be established with the Base or Area Commander to provide EOA support. The CEOM responsibilities are identified below in paragraph 3003.

4. <u>Battalion/Squadron Level Commanders</u>. Battalion/Squadron level commanders will designate, in writing, an Equal Opportunity Representative (EOR). The

EOR must be an officer or SNCO. A volunteer would be the ideal candidate; however, the commander must ensure the candidate is fully capable of dealing with issues that may be sensitive in nature. Commanders will ensure the EOR assignment does not create a conflict of interest with other duty assignments, i.e., XO, SgtMaj, Legal Officer or 1stSgt. Commands that have sub-units far removed from their major headquarters should consider designating a sub-unit EOR to help manage their EO objectives. It is highly recommended that sub-unit EORs also be assigned at the company level and in large work sections. These sub-unit EORs may be corporals and sergeants.

5. Commands listed in Appendix B are required to submit an annual Equal Opportunity Data Summary Report. The report will cover the period 1 October through 30 September and must arrive at CMC (MPE) by 15 November. The information required and the format for this report are contained in Appendix C.

3003. CEOM

1. The CEOM shall be an officer or SNCO designated to manage the commander's EO Program. The CEOM will normally:

    a. Monitor EOR assignments and ensure all subordinate unit EORs are assigned, trained and certified in accordance with chapter 4 of this Manual.

    b. Ensure all subordinate commands maintain and submit all reports required by this Manual.

    c. Provide assistance to the EOA in organizing and scheduling commander, senior enlisted, and EOR training.

    d. Be assigned to the billet for a minimum of one year.

    e. Attend quarterly EO sustainment training provided by the local EOA.

2. CEOMs will attend either the EO Program Managers Course (EOPMC) conducted at the DEOMI or local EOR Course (EORC) training. Limited seats for the DEOMI course are available through CMC (MPE); however, this training is unit funded.

3004. EOR

1. EORs are a vital part of the EO climate. These Marines are the central focus to ensuring the command's EO objectives are successful. Upon designation, EOR(s) will:

    a. Be assigned to the billet for a minimum of one year.

    b. Attend indoctrination training, EORC training, and quarterly EO sustainment training provided by a local EOA.

2. EORs assist commanders in establishing complaint procedures, reviewing complaints, assessing the command climate, and identifying and conducting equal opportunity training. EORs may assist the commanding officer in the maintenance and submission of required reports, in addition to conducting a review of command policy and action utilizing the Inspector General checklist

in Appendix H.   EORs may also be designated to conduct periodic reviews of the command's discrimination/sexual harassment complaint process as outlined in Appendix I.   EORs do not function as advocates for complainants and should not under normal circumstances conduct inquiries or investigations, but rather provide a source of information to both the complainant and the commander.   EORs are also points of contact for the local commands to request materials from the TIR Library managed by the nearest EOA.

3.   EORs shall provide EO training to all unit personnel and coordinate the training of additional instructors, if necessary.   They will ensure that all annual EO training identified in paragraph 4001 of this Manual is accomplished.

3005. EOA

1.   EOAs are assigned to commanders at major Marine Corps installations. Their mission is to provide instruction, assistance and advice on all EO matters.   Details on EOA responsibilities are located in MCO 5354.3 (Equal Opportunity Advisor).

2.   EOAs attend the EOA Resident Course (15 weeks) at DEOMI.   The course provides information related to EO program management, multicultural history, diversity, discrimination (includes sexual harassment), and training management.

3.   Recognizing that command structures are different, the commander has the prerogative of placing the EOA where he/she can best serve the needs of the command while maintaining access to the commander.

CHAPTER 4

EO TRAINING

CHAPTER 4

EO TRAINING

4000. GENERAL

1. The Marine Corps considers EO training as a part of basic leadership development. EO, in this view, is a combination of three leadership principles: (1) Know your Marines and look out for their welfare, (2) Set the example, and (3) Train your Marines as a team.

4001. TRAINING REQUIREMENTS. Commanders determine how best to accomplish EO training and must ensure it meets the requirements of this Manual and their command. The best method to conduct effective EO training is through small group discussions, with the EOR and/or EOA acting as a facilitator. The training should be imbedded in leadership development, and there should be personal involvement by the commander. Required training consists of the following:

1. **Equal Opportunity Policy Awareness Training.** All commands, to include PME and formal schools, will ensure EO is included in indoctrination training. Awareness training consists of an overview of the command's EO policies and procedures, to include EO complaint processing, and the Informal Resolution System (IRS). During awareness training, personnel shall be provided information on how to contact the command's EOR, CEOM, and EOA. Personnel shall also be provided with the EO hotline number and an explanation for its use.

2. **Annual EO Training.** All Marine Corps personnel will receive at a minimum one hour annually of training that details the Marine Corps EO policy; the effects of discrimination and sexual harassment on the individual Marine, the unit, and how discrimination undermines morale and mission accomplishment; and the proper use of the IRS. Commanders are encouraged to tailor the training to meet specific command needs and to use as much time as is required to ensure personnel are thoroughly familiar with the Marine Corps' EO policy. Other suggested areas for training are:

    a. **EO Leadership Awareness.** This training consists of Marine Corps and command policies, the forms of discrimination to include sexual harassment, identification of behaviors, personnel responsibilities, and characteristics of a hostile work environment.

    b. **Complaint Procedures.** This training explains the methods to seek resolution of EO issues. It shall identify and explain the formal and informal complaint procedures; the Informal Resolution System; selecting the best method for filing complaints; how and when you file an Article 138 UCMJ or Navy Regulations Article 1150; what must occur when a complaint is filed; how to address reprisal; an explanation of the complaint timelines; and other external methods to seek redress. The training shall also address the issue of filing false complaints.

    c. **Team Marine.** Team Marine is a training package in which Marines learn that equal opportunity issues are dealt with using leadership and our Core Values.

3. <u>Leadership Training</u>. Commanders are encouraged to include the principles of equal opportunity in SNCO and officer professional military education sessions. Only by such actions will the importance of equal opportunity and how it strengthens our leadership abilities be fully understood. Such training should stress to Marines how to build and maintain professional working relations and how fairness and unbiased actions are part of our Core Values. Instruction in PME Schools should be appropriate to the rank and experience of the students.

4. <u>EO Awareness Education</u>. Progressive EO training commensurate with rank will enable Marines in supervisory positions to recognize and resolve possible discriminatory and sexual harassment practices at the lowest level. The progressive levels of training are:

   a. <u>Command-Sponsored Corporal's Course</u>. The focus should be educating the small unit leader on awareness of cultural biases through socialization and perceptions. Suggested topics include Team Marine, Informal Resolution System (IRS), Sexual Harassment and Discrimination, and Request Mast.

   b. <u>Sergeant's Course</u>. The focus should be on skill development through effective communications. Suggested topics include Effective Listening Techniques, Complaint Processing Procedures, and Request Mast.

   c. <u>Career Course</u>. The focus should be on skill development through conflict resolution. Suggested topics include Filing Equal Opportunity (EO) Complaints; Role of the Equal Opportunity Representative (EOR); the Role of the Equal Opportunity Advisor (EOA); and Effective Use of Request Mast.

   d. <u>Advanced Course</u>. The focus should be on EO policy, senior/subordinate relationships, and discrimination. Suggested topics include EO Investigations and potential punishment imposed on sexual harassment and discrimination cases.

   e. <u>Officer Candidates School</u>. This training provides an introduction to Marine Corps policy on EO; sexual harassment and discrimination; leader's responsibilities; and IRS. The total period of instruction will be 2.0 hours.

   f. <u>The Basic School</u>. This training will focus on discrimination and sexual harassment, the effects of EO issues on the command, use of the IRS, Commanding Officer's responsibilities, and familiarization of standard terms in accordance with SECNAVINST 5300.26. The period of instruction is 3.0 hours.

4002. <u>EOR AND CEOM TRAINING</u>. EORs and CEOMs must attend local EOR training conducted by an EOA or be a graduate of the DEOMI 6-week EOPMC. This training is designed to prepare EORs and CEOMs to manage the command EO objectives for their commander. Local EOR/CEOM training shall consist of the following:

1. <u>Indoctrination Training</u>. Indoctrination training is designed to stress upon EORs/CEOMs the importance of EO, and ensure full understanding of the objectives. EO training shall consist of an overview of EOR/CEOM responsibilities, an understanding of equal opportunity and an introduction to this Manual. Indoctrination training shall be conducted by an EOA within 30 days of the assignment of the EOR/CEOM.

2. <u>EOR Course</u>. This training consists of 40 consecutive hours providing an in-depth review of all EO elements and thoroughly prepares EORs and CEOMs to manage their command's program. This training shall be completed within 90 days of assignment as an EOR/CEOM.

3. <u>Quarterly EOR/CEOM Sustainment Training</u>. All EORs and CEOMs shall regularly attend quarterly sustainment training conducted by an EOA. This training shall be used to reinforce the EO objectives, provide EO objectives update, and examine command trends.

4003. <u>COMMANDERS TRAINING</u>. Commanders (company through regimental/group level) are encouraged to attend a 3-day Commanders EO training course. Commander training is conducted by a local EOA and can be staggered to meet command needs.

4004. <u>SENIOR ENLISTED TRAINING</u>. Senior enlisted (MSgt/1stSgt/MGySgt/SgtMaj) training may be conducted by a local EOA and tailored to meet command needs. Senior enlisted personnel may also consider attending the one week Senior Enlisted EO Workshop at DEOMI. A limited number of seats for the workshop are available through CMC (MPE); however, the training is unit funded. Both courses are designed to stress upon senior enlisted how EO issues impact unit cohesion, mission accomplishment, and combat readiness.

4005. <u>EQUAL OPPORTUNITY ADVISOR SUSTAINMENT TRAINING</u>. In an attempt to sustain the EOA's knowledge of the EO program and increase their effectiveness, it is recommended that EOAs continue to seek training whenever possible. The following training is recommended for all EOAs:

1. DoD Worldwide Equal Opportunity Conference

2. Marine Corps EOA Conference(s)

3. DEOMI Mediation Training

4. Inspector General Investigation Training

4006. <u>CULTURAL AWARENESS TRAINING</u>. Recognition of various cultural/gender awareness/remembrance periods is required by reference (a). It is left to the commander's discretion as to how this recognition is to be accomplished, although some form of acknowledgment must be accomplished during the mandated observance periods. Commanders may elect to conduct a combined multicultural event instead of numerous individual cultural events. Commanders are encouraged to establish EO councils to plan observance strategies and involve command personnel. Cultural awareness training that does not build unity, understanding, and teamwork, is contrary to the intent of this requirement.

4007. <u>DEOMI MOBILE TRAINING TEAMS (MTT)</u>. Commanders may request an MTT from DEOMI to conduct EO training specifically designed to meet the needs of the requesting command. MTT's are unit funded and may be requested per the procedures listed in Appendix K.

CHAPTER 5

PROCESSING/REPORTING EO COMPLAINTS

CHAPTER 5

PROCESSING/REPORTING EO COMPLAINTS

5000. GENERAL. An EO complaint is a report of conduct that is known or suspected to be discriminatory in nature, based on age, color, gender, race, religion, or national origin. (Sexual harassment is a form discrimination. See paragraph 2009). Reporting procedures are established to provide each individual a means to seek redress of any known or suspected acts of discrimination. All commands are required to understand and adhere to the procedures and timelines established in this Manual.

5001. PROTECTED COMMUNICATION. All EO complaints are sensitive in nature and shall be classified as protected communication. EO complaints identified to the chain of command may include, but are not limited to, those presented during Request Mast or NJP. Participation of a witness during an official investigation also qualifies as protected communication. Also, communications received by third parties, i.e., spouse, relative, co-worker, IG, a Member of Congress, or any designated official are to be considered protected communications. Appendix F provides the complete definition of protected communication.

1. Privacy Act. All equal opportunity complaints will be handled in accordance with the Privacy Act. Any complaint that has not been resolved shall be restricted to personnel with a need to know. Individual privacy, to the maximum extent possible, must be protected through all stages of the investigation and resolution of the complaint. This is not only required by the Privacy Act of 1974 and SECNAVINST 5300.26, but is also necessary if all personnel are to have trust in their command's handling of EO issues. Once a complaint has been resolved, commanders may release certain information, in accordance with the Privacy Act, to publicize the consequences of unlawful discrimination.

2. Security of Information. All EO complaints shall be maintained in a secure location that restricts and limits access. Agencies or individuals wishing copies of a case resolution shall submit a formal request to the commanding officer that directed the investigation. Commanding officers shall provide information or copies to those agencies or individuals who have a lawful requirement for access. All other requests must be submitted in accordance with the Freedom Of Information Act (FOIA). Commands shall maintain copies of completed cases for a minimum of 2 years.

5002. METHODS TO ADDRESS INAPPROPRIATE BEHAVIOR. There are two methods to address inappropriate behavior, informal and formal. The circumstances involved will determine the appropriate method to address complaints.

1. Informal. This method uses the Informal Resolution System (IRS), NAVPERS 15620, to resolve a conflict that is less than criminal in nature. The IRS is comprised of three sections: behavior zones (Red, Yellow, and Green), roles of those involved (Recipient, Offending Person, Other Person, and Supervisor), and resolutions (Direct, Informal Third Party, and Training Information Resources). It emphasizes each person's responsibility to be a role model of appropriate behavior and to confront any form of discrimination, harassment, or other inappropriate behavior when it is

observed or brought to their attention. When inappropriate behavior occurs due to differing views, different personalities, lack of understanding, miscommunication, or stereotypes, the IRS is one of the most effective methods to resolve the conflict. The IRS may be used if the complainant agrees to it. This is the complainant's decision, not the commander's. When using the IRS, no formal action is required by the command; however, the commander if deemed necessary may take additional action. Personnel should always consider using the informal method whenever possible, as this is the most expeditious means to attempt resolution and restore the trust necessary for unit cohesion. Appendix E of this Manual contains a detailed description of the IRS, to include the commander's responsibilities under the IRS.

2. Formal. This method is used to seek a formal resolution to a complaint of inappropriate behavior. Formal allegations can only be resolved by the commander. Anyone within the chain of command who receives a formal complaint will forward the complaint immediately to the commander. All formal complaints will be reported to the CMC, via the DASH, even when IRS is utilized. Installation EOAs will assist commanders in submitting DASH reports. If an EOA is not located in your geographical area, contact CMC (MPE) for further guidance.

5003. AVENUES TO FILE FORMAL COMPLAINTS. There are several avenues to seek formal redress. The most effective avenue to use will depend upon the circumstances surrounding the situation and personnel involved. Selection of the avenue to use will be decided by the complainant.

1. Request Mast. This is the preferred method for an individual to file a formal complaint of discrimination, to include sexual harassment. The Request Mast will normally be conducted within one working day, but no later than three working days, after the initial submission. MCO 1700.23, Request Mast, provides specific guidance for Request Mast procedures. A copy of the Request Mast form is provided in Appendix M.

2. Article 138, UCMJ Complaint. An individual who alleges wrong(s) committed by their Commanding Officer may file a formal complaint under Article 138, UCMJ. Commanders should consult with the staff judge advocate (SJA) when processing a complaint under Article 138.

3. Article 1150, Redress of Wrong(s) Committed by a Superior. An individual may also file a complaint against any other superior, in rank or command, who the individual believes committed a wrongdoing (U.S. Navy Regulations, Article 1150). Commanders should consult with the SJA when processing a complaint under Article 1150.

4. Communications With Inspectors General. As an alternative to the normal chain of command, military and civilian personnel may lodge complaints and provide facts to the local Command Inspector. Complaints may be lodged with representatives of the Deputy Naval Inspector General or to representatives of the Deputy Naval Inspector General for Marine Corps Matters/Inspector General of the Marine Corps (DNIGMC), DSN 224-1348/49 or commercial (703) 614-1348/49, concerning violations of laws, rules, and regulations; abuse of authority; or other misconduct.

5. Individual Communications With Congress. Individuals may write a personal letter to members of Congress at anytime concerning EO issues.

5004. INITIATION OF AN EO COMPLAINT

1. Any person may report suspected cases of discrimination to supervisors in the chain of command. In such cases, a thorough inquiry/investigation into the complaint is required. An EO complaint may be made orally, in writing, or both. Regardless of who initially receives the complaint, it must be forwarded immediately to the proper authority (normally the immediate commanding officer of the offending person).

2. Initiating a complaint is not the same as preferring charges. Preferring charges is the separate function of signing and swearing to charges in preparation for courts-martial or NJP.

5005. COMPLAINT INVESTIGATION AND ACTION

1. It is the responsibility of the commanding officer of the alleged offender to conduct a thorough investigation and take appropriate action. It is the responsibility of the command in which the complaint was received to ensure a DASH report is initiated. For complaints involving personnel from other commands and geographic locations it will require close coordination between commands to achieve resolution. The offender's command shall provide the complainant's commander with a copy of the completed investigation, to include actions taken. If a commander is unable to resolve the case, he or she may forward the case to a higher command for resolution. Complainants will be advised of the progress of the investigation every 14 days.

2. Complaints involving other than Marine Corps/Marine Corps civilian personnel will be reported to the individual's commanding officer (Active Duty Military) or supervisor (DoD/civilian) or contact the CMC (MPE) for guidance. Complaints involving civilian contractors will be reported to the contracting company, via the Commanding Officer of the complainant. Commanding Officers may be required to conduct investigations on personnel involved in incidents that did not occur at their command or include other Service members in order to assist other Service branches or contracting companies.

3. Complaints involving Flag/General Officers or Senior Executive Service personnel will be referred to the DNIGMC for investigation.

5006. FORMAL COMPLAINT PROCEDURES. Any formal EO complaint or allegation of discrimination on the basis of age, color, gender, race, religion, national origin or any other form of unlawful discrimination, to include sexual harassment, shall utilize the procedures established within this Manual. Commanders must make every effort to adhere to the timeline identified.

1. All formal complaints should be filed (registered) within 60 days of the alleged incident occurring by the person making the allegation.

2. Within 72 hours or three working days of a commander receiving a formal complaint or notification of a formal complaint, the command must initiate an investigation into the allegation(s). If the formal complaint is against the commander, the complaint must be referred to the next higher command for resolution. If the formal complaint is against Flag/General Officers or Senior Executive Service personnel, the complaint will be forwarded to the DNIGMC for resolution.

3. Also within 72 hours or three working days, a detailed description of the allegation(s) shall be forwarded in writing via the chain of command to the officer in the chain of command who has general court-martial convening authority (GCMCA). This report must include the name of the assigned investigator.

4. The commander shall inform the complainant when the investigation has commenced and make every effort to ensure the investigation is completed within 14 days of commencement.

5. Upon completion of the investigation, the investigating officer shall ensure a legal sufficiency review and an EO review is conducted on the findings and recommendations. The SJA will conduct the legal review. The investigating officer will then submit the investigation to the commander, and the commander will provide the investigation to the EOA. This will enable the EOA to advise the commander on the EO sufficiency of the investigation as well. If an EOA is not geographically located with the unit, contact CMC (MPE) for guidance.

6. If the investigation and required reviews are not completed within 14 days, the command will submit a written request for extension from the Commanding General with GCMCA. The request must report on the progress made to complete the investigation and the purpose for the extension. The Commanding General can authorize only 30 days of extension. If an investigation cannot be completed after a 30-day extension the command must contact CMC (MPE).

7. The commander has 6 days upon completion of the investigation and review to forward a final written report containing the results of the investigation, as well as any action taken, to the next superior officer in the chain of command with GCMCA. The report will include a statement from the complainant that indicates their satisfaction or dissatisfaction with the resolution. The complainant resolution statement should be taken by the EOA or EOR after notification of resolution.

8. Upon completion of the commander's final written report, a final DASH report will be submitted to CMC (MPE), in accordance with paragraph 5007. For the purpose of a final DASH report, a complaint is considered final when the investigation is complete and the commander makes the determination as to the validity (substantiated or unsubstantiated) of the complaint.

9. Throughout the investigation, updates and feedback will be provided to the complainant every 14 days.

10. If the case is referred to NJP, court-martial and/or administrative separation proceeding, CMC (MPE) will be updated via DASH report of the outcome. (Note: The outcome of court-martial proceedings does not change the closure code within the DASH report).

5007. DISCRIMINATION AND SEXUAL HARASSMENT (DASH) REPORTS

1. Due to the sensitivity of discrimination and sexual harassment complaints, CMC (MPE) has implemented the DASH complaint tracking system. The DASH report is required when a formal complaint is filed and a Marine is involved. The purpose of the DASH system is to track all formal complaints of discrimination or sexual harassment and the parties involved in the

investigation until final action is taken. It is a tool to assist in ensuring that all EO complaints are appropriately addressed. It is not a report card for units, commanders, or installations. The information is used primarily to provide statistical data for reports and to assist in identifying trends (both positive and negative) on the EO climate of the Marine Corps. The information gathered requires a number of personal entries; therefore, appropriate measures must be taken to ensure the security of all information entered into the database. Access to information will be restricted to those with a need to know only. DASH reports are required to identify the following:

    a. Initial Report. This report is required to identify an allegation of discrimination against a Marine. It indicates the initiation of an investigation by the command(s) involved and that an investigator has been assigned.

    b. Continuation. This report is required if an EO investigation cannot be completed within the prescribed timelines. A 30-day extension can be authorized by the general officer with GCMCA. The reason for the extension must be included in the report.

    c. Final. This report is required to identify that an EO investigation has been completed and final disposition has been rendered.

    d. Update. This report is required to update the status of disposition in an EO complaint when a Marine is recommended for NJP or court-martial. This report does not change the final closure code.

2. Local Reports. The DASH reporting format is not intended to be used to inform the chain of command of allegations of discrimination. Restriction on the use of personal information at the local level will help to ensure the confidentiality and security of the reporting process.

3. When a DASH Report is Not Required. Formal allegations of discrimination presented to Marine Corps commanders require the involvement of the immediate commanders and their staffs to resolve the complaint. Yet, the Marine Corps DASH reporting requirements are not applicable when:

    a. Incidents Involve Only Civilian Personnel. EEO cases are reported through the appropriate civilian EEO procedures, utilizing MCO 12713.5.

    b. Alleged Complaints Do Not Include Marine Corps Military Members. Military members who are assigned to Marine Corps installations, (i.e., Naval hospital staff, dental corps) shall at times require an investigation be conducted by the commander to assist the parent Service in resolving an EO issue. Such an investigation does not require DASH reporting.

4. DASH Reporting Procedures

    a. It is the responsibility of the command in which the complaint was received to ensure a DASH report is initiated. The DASH report is required when a formal complaint is filed and a Marine is the complainant or alleged offender. The command that receives the complaint is responsible for ensuring a DASH report is submitted to the CMC (MPE).

b. Within 20 days after the date on which the investigation commenced, commanders are required to submit a DASH report, using the format in Appendix D. The report will include the name of the investigator and date assigned.

(1) Commanders will notify the CMC (MPE) of the status of the complaint using the DASH report format contained in Appendix D. The command EOA will provide advice on DASH report submission procedures.

(2) Multiple allegations of inappropriate behavior or wrongdoing may be presented to the commander. Therefore, when preparing the DASH report, commanders will provide only the information and action taken that is relevant to the alleged behavior that is considered discrimination/harassment as defined by this Manual.

(3) DASH update reports will be submitted by the commander. The commander is responsible for ensuring the update report is submitted to CMC (MPE), with assistance from the command EOA. Updates are required upon receiving an extension, upon determination for disposition or resolution, upon conclusion of NJP, court-martial or other administrative action not previously reported. Commands not located at or near an installation with an EOA need to contact Headquarters, U.S. Marine Corps (MPE), 3280 Russell Road, Quantico, VA 22134-5103, commercial phone number (703) 784-9371, DSN 278-9371 for further guidance. DASH reports should not be reported via message traffic due to the sensitive nature of the information and to protect the privacy of the people involved.

(4) If an extension is granted, commands will ensure the narrative section of the DASH report includes the reason(s) for the extension, length of the extension, and the name of the commanding general authorizing the extension.

(5) Final DASH reports will be appended to the 'closed' incident case files and maintained by the command that originated the DASH report. Closed case information is to be maintained by the command for 2 years with restricted access.

c. The offender's commander shall ensure resolution information is provided to the complainant's commander for a final DASH input or update. The final report will include: the complainant resolution statement, a determination of validity of the charges, administrative action taken if any, and a recommendation for NJP or court-martial if warranted.

APPENDIX A

COMMAND MILITARY PERSONNEL RACE/ETHNIC STATISTICS REPORT FORMAT

(This report is not required to be submitted to HQMC. It is provided to assist commanders in managing their EO program.)

	See note 1	WHITE	AI/AN	ASIAN	B/AF	HISP	NH/OPI	TOTAL COMMAND
I	On-Board Strength							
	A. Number Males	___	___	___	___	___	___	___
	B. Number Females	___	___	___	___	___	___	___
	C. Percentage Males	___	___	___	___	___	___	___
	D. Percentage Females	___	___	___	___	___	___	___
II	Promotions (Data available in Marine Corps Total Force System (MCTFS))							
	A. To Sergeant							
	1. Males Eligible	___	___	___	___	___	___	___
	2. Females Eligible	___	___	___	___	___	___	___
	3. Males Not Recommended	___	___	___	___	___	___	___
	4. Females Not Recommended	___	___	___	___	___	___	___
	5. Males Selected	___	___	___	___	___	___	___
	6. Females Selected	___	___	___	___	___	___	___
	7. Percentage Males	___	___	___	___	___	___	___
	8. Percentage Females	___	___	___	___	___	___	___
	B. To Corporal							
	1. Males Eligible	___	___	___	___	___	___	___
	2. Females Eligible	___	___	___	___	___	___	___
	3. Males Not Recommended	___	___	___	___	___	___	___
	4. Females Not Recommended	___	___	___	___	___	___	___
	5. Males Selected	___	___	___	___	___	___	___
	6. Females Selected	___	___	___	___	___	___	___
	7. Percentage Males	___	___	___	___	___	___	___
	8. Percentage Females	___	___	___	___	___	___	___
	C. To Lance Corporal							
	1. Males Eligible	___	___	___	___	___	___	___
	2. Females Eligible	___	___	___	___	___	___	___
	3. Males Not Recommended	___	___	___	___	___	___	___
	4. Females Not Recommended	___	___	___	___	___	___	___

See note 1	WHITE	AI/AN	ASIAN	B/AF	HISP	NH/OPI	TOTAL COMMAND
5. Males Selected	___	___	___	___	___	___	___
6. Females Selected	___	___	___	___	___	___	___
7. Percentage Males	___	___	___	___	___	___	___
8. Percentage Females	___	___	___	___	___	___	___

III   Recognition (Data available in MCTFS)

   A. Medals

1. Males Awarded	___	___	___	___	___	___	___
2. Females Awarded	___	___	___	___	___	___	___

   B. Certificates of Commendation/Meritorious Masts

1. Males Awarded	___	___	___	___	___	___	___
2. Females Awarded	___	___	___	___	___	___	___

IV   Formal Discrimination/Harassment Complaints

   A. Male (# Reported)

1. Discrimination	___	___	___	___	___	___	___
2. Sexual Harassment	___	___	___	___	___	___	___

   B. Female (# Reported)

1. Discrimination	___	___	___	___	___	___	___
2. Sexual Harassment	___	___	___	___	___	___	___

V   Disciplinary Actions (Data available in MCTFS)

   A. NJP (Total)

1. Males	___	___	___	___	___	___	___
2. Females	___	___	___	___	___	___	___

   B. Court-Martial

1. Males	___	___	___	___	___	___	___
2. Females	___	___	___	___	___	___	___

VI   Admin Discharges (Prior to Normal EAS/ECC) (Data available in MCTFS)

   A. Honorable

1. Males	___	___	___	___	___	___	___
2. Females	___	___	___	___	___	___	___

   B. General

1. Males	___	___	___	___	___	___	___
2. Females	___	___	___	___	___	___	___

   C. Other Than Honorable

1. Males	___	___	___	___	___	___	___

See note 1	WHITE	AI/AN	ASIAN	B/AF	HISP	NH/OPI	TOTAL COMMAND
2. Females	____	____	____	____	____	____	____

D. Bad Conduct

	WHITE	AI/AN	ASIAN	B/AF	HISP	NH/OPI	TOTAL COMMAND
1. Males	____	____	____	____	____	____	____
2. Females	____	____	____	____	____	____	____

E. Dishonorable

	WHITE	AI/AN	ASIAN	B/AF	HISP	NH/OPI	TOTAL COMMAND
1. Males	____	____	____	____	____	____	____
2. Females	____	____	____	____	____	____	____

VII Medical Discharges (Prior to Normal EAS/ECC) (Data available in MCTFS)

	WHITE	AI/AN	ASIAN	B/AF	HISP	NH/OPI	TOTAL COMMAND
A. Males	____	____	____	____	____	____	____
B. Females	____	____	____	____	____	____	____

VIII Reenlistments (Data available in MCTFS)

A. Eligible

	WHITE	AI/AN	ASIAN	B/AF	HISP	NH/OPI	TOTAL COMMAND
1. Males	____	____	____	____	____	____	____
2. Females	____	____	____	____	____	____	____

B. Recommended

	WHITE	AI/AN	ASIAN	B/AF	HISP	NH/OPI	TOTAL COMMAND
1. Males	____	____	____	____	____	____	____
2. Females	____	____	____	____	____	____	____

C. Not Recommended

	WHITE	AI/AN	ASIAN	B/AF	HISP	NH/OPI	TOTAL COMMAND
1. Males	____	____	____	____	____	____	____
2. Females	____	____	____	____	____	____	____

IX Training completed during this reporting period (Data available in MCTFS)

A. MASP (Military Academic Skills Program)

	WHITE	AI/AN	ASIAN	B/AF	HISP	NH/OPI	TOTAL COMMAND
1. Percentage Males	____	____	____	____	____	____	____
2. Percentage Females	____	____	____	____	____	____	____

B. Corporals Course

	WHITE	AI/AN	ASIAN	B/AF	HISP	NH/OPI	TOTAL COMMAND
1. Percentage Males	____	____	____	____	____	____	____
2. Percentage Females	____	____	____	____	____	____	____

C. Sergeants Course

	WHITE	AI/AN	ASIAN	B/AF	HISP	NH/OPI	TOTAL COMMAND
1. Percentage Males	____	____	____	____	____	____	____
2. Percentage Females	____	____	____	____	____	____	____

D. SNCO Career Course

	WHITE	AI/AN	ASIAN	B/AF	HISP	NH/OPI	TOTAL COMMAND
1. Percentage Males	____	____	____	____	____	____	____

See note 1	WHITE	AI/AN	ASIAN	B/AF	HISP	NH/OPI	TOTAL COMMAND
2. Percentage Females	____	____	____	____	_____	_____	_____

E. SNCO Advanced Course

	WHITE	AI/AN	ASIAN	B/AF	HISP	NH/OPI	TOTAL COMMAND
1. Percentage Males	____	____	____	____	_____	_____	_____
2. Percentage Females	____	____	____	____	_____	_____	_____

X   EO Training Conducted

	WHITE	AI/AN	ASIAN	B/AF	HISP	NH/OPI	TOTAL COMMAND
A. Males	____	____	____	____	_____	_____	_____
B. Females	____	____	____	____	_____	_____	_____

Notes: (1) Abbreviations for Race/Ethnic Identifiers
         (AI/AN)   American Indian/Alaska Native
         (A)   Asian
         (NH/OPI)   Native Hawaiian/Other Pacific Islander
         (B/AF)   Black/African American
         (H)   Hispanic/Latino
         (W)   White

APPENDIX B

COMMANDS REQUIRED TO SUBMIT AN ANNUAL EQUAL OPPORTUNITY DATA SUMMARY REPORT

The below listed commands are required to submit an annual Equal Opportunity Data Summary Report to CMC (MPE). The report provides Commanding Officer and Executive Officer assignments by race and gender, utilizing the format in Appendix C.

Commander, Marine Forces Pacific/COMMARCORBASESPAC *

Commander, Marine Forces Atlantic/COMMARCORBASESLANT *

Commander, Marine Forces Reserve *

Commanding General, Marine Corps Combat Development Command **

Commander, Marine Corps Materiel Command

Commanding General, Marine Corps Recruiting Command

Commanding General, Marine Corps National Capital Region

NOTE: * Reserve units shall submit one report on active duty personnel and a separate report on reserve personnel.

          ** Do not include personnel undergoing training

APPENDIX C

ANNUAL EQUAL OPPORTUNITY DATA SUMMARY REPORT FORMAT

The purpose of this report is to enable HQMC to provide data annually to the Military Equal Opportunity Assessment. This data is not available through other sources like the Total Force Data Warehouse. Accordingly, the commanders identified in Appendix B are requested to provide it each year to CMC (MPE) by 15 November.

	CO		XO	
	Male	Female	Male	Female
American Indian/Alaska Native	_____	_____	_____	_____
Asian	_____	_____	_____	_____
Native Hawaiian/Other Pacific Islander	_____	_____	_____	_____
Black/African American	_____	_____	_____	_____
Hispanic/Latino	_____	_____	_____	_____
White	_____	_____	_____	_____

APPENDIX D

USMC DISCRIMINATION AND SEXUAL HARASSMENT (DASH) REPORT TO CMC (MPE) Part 1 of 5

The major command will notify the CMC (MPE) via DASH within 20 days of an immediate commander receiving a formal report or allegation of discrimination, to include sexual harassment. The complaint will be entered into DASH by the installation EO Advisor. The format for the INITIAL DASH report is contained in the following five part form. LEAVE DATA ELEMENTS BLANK WHEN INFORMATION IS UNAVAILABLE OR DETERMINATION HAS NOT BEEN MADE. After filing an INITIAL DASH report with CMC (MPE), use Part 1A (DASH Status Update Report) to provide further update and/or to report FINAL closure of this incident.

1. INCIDENT DESCRIPTION   DATE INITIATED:

(A) INCIDENT NUMBER: (B) DATE REPORTED:

(C) REPORT TYPE: ☐ Initial   ☐ Continuation   ☐ Final   (D) REPORTING SERVICE:

(E) UIC / MCC: (F) POC:
                    PHONE:
                    LOCATION:

(G) DATE(S) OF INCIDENT: (H) TYPE DISCRIMINATION:
  From: ☐ Age   ☐ Sex   ☐ Religion   ☐ Race   ☐ Sexual Harassment
  To: Other:

(I) LOCATION: (J) REPORTED THROUGH

(K) SENSITIVITY

(L) DESCRIPTION OF INCIDENT:

Incident No: Date Printed: Page 1

USMC DISCRIMINATION AND SEXUAL HARASSMENT (DASH) REPORT TO CMC (MPE) Part 2 of 5

PRIVACY ACT STATEMENT   Requiring Document: MCO P5354.1D, Marine Corps Equal Opportunity Manual. Sponsor Code: CMC(MPE).   Authority: Title 5 U.S. Code 301; Title 10. Privacy Act of 1974, as amended by Title 5 U.S. Code 522a. Principal Purpose: Statistical data collection and tracking of complaints received. Routine uses: Used to track the resolution of complaints and/or allegations of discrimination or sexual harassment. received by a unit through formal reporting channels. Disclosure: Disclosure of the requested information. is voluntary. Failure to disclose the requested information. may result in delay of the resolution process or inhibit the ability of the command to effectively process the complaint. and promote the goals of the Marine Corps Equal Opportunity Program.

Signature of this Recipient: Date:

2. RECIPIENT INFORMATION: (REPEAT FOR EACH RECIPIENT)		DATE INITIATED:
(A) RECIPIENT NUMBER: of	(B) COMPONENT:	(C) PAY GRADE:
(D) GENDER:	(E) RACE/ETHNICITY:	(F) ALCOHOL USE SUSPECTED:

(G) RECIPIENT PERSONAL INFORMATION: (REQUIRES PRIVACY ACT STATEMENT TO BE SIGNED BY RECIPIENT)		
(1) LAST NAME:	(2) FIRST NAME:	(3) MIDDLE INITIAL:
(4) SSN:	(5) DATE OF BIRTH:	
(6) LOCAL ADDRESS:		
(7) CITY:	(8) STATE:	(9) ZIP CODE: -
(10) COML PHONE:	(11) DSN PHONE:	(12) MARITAL STATUS:
(13) RELIGION:		(14) MILITARY/CIVILIAN:

(H) RECIPIENT MILITARY INFORMATION:		
(1) MAJOR COMMAND: (NAME)	(2) GRADE: (CORPORAL, ETC.)	(3) MOS:
(4) STATUS:	(5) DUTY STATUS AT TIME OF INCIDENT:	(6) ACTIVE DUTY SERVICE DATE:
(7) ROTATION DATE:	(8) EAS:	(9) UIC/RUC:
(10) FUTURE MCC:	(11) CO NAME / GRADE:	
(12) CO PHONE NUMBER:		

INCIDENT NO:	Date Printed:	Page 1

USMC DISCRIMINATION AND SEXUAL HARASSMENT (DASH) REPORT TO CMC (MPE) Part 3 of 5

PRIVACY ACT STATEMENT Requiring Document: MCO P5354.1D, Marine Corps Equal Opportunity Manual. Sponsor Code: CMC(MPE). Authority: Title 5 U.S. Code 301; Title 10. Privacy Act of 1974, as amended by Title 5 U.S. Code 522a. Principal Purpose: Statistical data collection and tracking of complaints received. Routine uses: Used to track the resolution of complaints and/or allegations of discrimination or sexual harassment received by a unit through formal reporting channels. Disclosure: Disclosure of the requested information is voluntary. Failure to disclose the requested information may result in delay of the resolution process or inhibit the ability of the command to effectively process the complaint and promote the goals of the Marine Corps Equal Opportunity Program.

Signature of this Alleged Offender: Date:

3. ALLEGED OFFENDER INFORMATION: (REPEAT FOR EACH ALLEGED OFFENDER)		DATE INITIATED:
(A) ALLEGED OFFENDER NUMBER: of	(B) COMPONENT:	(C) PAY GRADE:
(D) GENDER:	(E) RACE/ETHNICITY:	(F) RELATIONSHIP TO RECIPIENT:
(G) ALCOHOL USE SUSPECTED:		

(H) ALLEGED OFFENDER PERSONAL INFORMATION: (REQUIRES PRIVACY ACT STATEMENT TO BE SIGNED BY ALLEGED OFFENDER)		
(1) LAST NAME:	(2) FIRST NAME:	(3) MIDDLE INITIAL:
(4) SSN:	(5) DATE OF BIRTH: (YYYYMMDD)	
(6) LOCAL ADDRESS:		
(7) CITY:	(8) STATE:	(9) ZIP CODE: -
(10) COML PHONE:	(11) DSN PHONE:	(12) MARITAL STATUS:
(13) RELIGION:		(14) MILITARY/CIVILIAN:

(I) ALLEGED OFFENDER MILITARY INFORMATION: (REQUIRES PRIVACY ACT STATEMENT TO BE SIGNED BY ALLEGED OFFENDER)		
(1) MAJOR COMMAND: (NAME)	(2) GRADE: (CORPORAL, ETC.)	(3) MOS:
(4) STATUS:	(5) DUTY STATUS AT TIME OF INCIDENT:	(6) ACTIVE DUTY SERVICE DATE:
(7) ROTATION DATE:	(8) EAS:	(9) UIC/RUC:
(10) FUTURE MCC:	(11) CO NAME / GRADE:	
(12) CO PHONE NUMBER:		

INCIDENT NO:	Date Printed:	Page 1

USMC DISCRIMINATION AND SEXUAL HARASSMENT (DASH) REPORT TO CMC (MPE) Part 4 of 5

4. INCIDENT DISPOSITION/RESOLUTION

DATE PREPARED:

REPEAT THIS PAGE FOR EACH ALLEGED OFFENDER:

ALLEGED OFFENDER'S NAME: (LAST, FIRST, MI)

(A) DATE ACTION COMPLETED:	(B) CLOSURE CODE: SUBSTAN/UNSUB

(C) ACTION TAKEN: ☐ ADMINISTRATIVE ☐ JUDICIAL

IF ADMINISTRATIVE: IF JUDICIAL:

NARRATIVE OF ADMINISTRATIVE ACTION TAKEN:

(D) JUDICIAL TRIAL RESULTS:

(E) MILITARY SENTENCE:

(F) CIVILIAN SENTENCE:

NARRATIVE OF MILITARY TRIAL / CIVILIAN RESULTS:
Military Results:

Civilian Results:

(G) CONVENING AUTHORITY APPROVAL:

NARRATIVE OF APPROVING AUTHORITY RESULTS, (IF REQUIRED):

INCIDENT NO: Date Printed: Page 2

USMC DISCRIMINATION AND SEXUAL HARASSMENT (DASH) REPORT TO CMC (MPE) Part 5 of 5

PRIVACY ACT STATEMENT   Requiring Document: MCO P5354.1D, Marine Corps Equal Opportunity Manual. Sponsor Code: CMC(MPE).   Authority: Title 5 U.S. Code 301; Title 10. Privacy Act of 1974, as amended by Title 5 U.S. Code 522a. Principal Purpose: Statistical data collection and tracking of complaints received. Routine uses: Used to track the resolution of complaints and/or allegations of discrimination or sexual harassment received by a unit through formal reporting channels. Disclosure: Disclosure of the requested information is voluntary. Failure to disclose the requested information may result in delay of the resolution process or inhibit the ability of the command to effectively process the complaint and promote the goals of the Marine Corps Equal Opportunity Program.

Signature of this Witness: Date:

5. WITNESS PERSONAL INFORMATION: (REPEAT FOR EACH WITNESS)	DATE INITIATED:
(A) WITNESS NUMBER:	of
(B) LAST NAME:	
(C) FIRST NAME:	
(D) MIDDLE INITIAL:	
(E) GENDER:	
(F) REQUESTS ANONYMITY:	
(G) COMPONENT:	
(H) GRADE: (CORPORAL, ETC.)	
(I) LOCAL ADDRESS:	
(J) CITY:	
(K) STATE / COUNTRY:	
(L) ZIP CODE:	-
(M) PHONE: (COML WORK)	
(N) DSN:	
(O) RELATIONSHIP TO RECIPIENT:	
(P) MILITARY/ CIVILIAN:	

LOCAL USE OF THIS SPACE TO RECORD SUMMARY BY THIS WITNESS: (NOT SENT TO CMC MPE)

INCIDENT NO: Date Printed: Page 1

USMC DISCRIMINATION AND SEXUAL HARASSMENT (DASH) REPORT TO CMC (MPE) Part 1A
STATUS UPDATE REPORT

Formal complaints or allegations not resolved during the initial 20 day period require additional action in accordance with chapter 5 of MCO P5354.1D. The format for these additional reports is listed below. Action is complete when all action, to include administrative separation processing has been completed, or the commander has determined the allegation to be unsubstantiated, or the alleged offender is found innocent at a courtmartial/civilian court. Final update status will also be submitted in the following format:

1. COMPLAINT IDENTIFIER

(A) INCIDENT NUMBER:

(B) TODAY'S DATE:

(C) REPORT TYPE: ☐ CONTINUATION   ☐ FINAL

(D) COMMAND POC:

PHONE:
LOCATION:

2. DISPOSITION INFORMATION   (REPEAT FOR EACH ALLEGED OFFENDER)

ALLEGED OFFENDER'S NAME: (LAST, FIRST, MI)

(A) DATE ACTION COMPLETED:

(B) CLOSURE CODE: SUBSTANTIATED/UNSUBSTANTIATED

(C) ACTION TAKEN: ☐ ADMINISTRATIVE   ☐ JUDICIAL

IF ADMINISTRATIVE: IF JUDICIAL:

NARRATIVE OF ADMINISTRATIVE ACTION TAKEN:

(D) JUDICIAL TRIAL RESULTS:

(E) MILITARY SENTENCE:

(F) CIVILIAN SENTENCE:

(G) NARRATIVE OF MILITARY TRIAL / CIVILIAN RESULTS:
   Military Results:

   Civilian Results:

(H) CONVENING AUTHORITY APPROVAL: No

NARRATIVE OF APPROVING AUTHORITY RESULTS, (IF REQUIRED):

(I) DATE FINAL ACTION COMPLETED:

INCIDENT NO:

APPENDIX E

INFORMAL RESOLUTION SYSTEM (IRS)

1. BACKGROUND. Development of the IRS was directed by SECNAV to facilitate resolution of interpersonal conflicts at the lowest possible level. It was developed to help resolve conflict resulting from any form of discrimination, to include sexual harassment, or other inappropriate behavior.

2. IRS CONCEPT AND GOALS. Provide necessary information and skills to encourage/facilitate resolving interpersonal conflicts in the workplace at the lowest possible level.

   a. Emphasizes core values: Honor, Courage, and Commitment.

   b. Emphasizes each person's responsibility to be role model of appropriate behavior and confront inappropriate behavior when observed or brought to his/her attention.

3. INDIVIDUAL RESPONSIBILITIES. In general, each individual's responsibilities are:

   a. Do not ignore discrimination, sexual harassment, or other inappropriate behavior when it is encountered or observed,

   b. Review options under the IRS, and

   c. Take action to resolve the conflict.

4. IRS IS COMPRISED OF THREE SECTIONS

   a. Behavior zones (based on "reasonable person" standard)

      (1) Red. Always unacceptable, e.g., seeking sexual favors in return for favorable evaluation, making supervisory decisions based on race/gender, and "hate" mail. The most severe forms of red zone behavior are clearly criminal, like rape, and assault.

         (a) Behavior that is criminal in nature cannot be resolved by using the IRS. Such behavior must be reported through appropriate law enforcement channels.

         (b) Non-criminal red zone, if resolved and recipient does not desire further action, should merely be reported and documented for supervisor's information.

      (2) Yellow. Inappropriate behavior. Racial/sexual slurs, comments, jokes, sexually suggestive touching. If repeated, especially after being told of its offensiveness, turns to red, and becomes definitely unacceptable.

      (3) Green. Acceptable. Includes counseling on performance or military appearance. Normal social interaction; polite compliment; touching which could not reasonably be perceived in a sexual or threatening way; and friendly conversation.

   b. Roles

      (1) Recipient. One who feels offended/harassed.

(2) <u>Offending person</u>. One who may have offended/harassed another.

(3) <u>Third party</u>. One approached by recipient or by offending person or who observes inappropriate behavior.

(4) <u>Supervisor</u>. Anyone who has subordinates, regardless of grade or rank, and who is approached by any of the above three (or who himself/herself observes inappropriate behavior).

   c. <u>Resolution Options (Under IRS)</u>

(1) <u>Direct</u>. Recipient attempts to resolve conflict directly with offending person. This is the preferred method of resolving conflict.

(2) <u>Informal Third Party</u>. Recipient (or offending person) enlists the informal assistance of some other person to help resolve the conflict.

(3) <u>Training Information Resources</u>. Generic, non-accusatory command training.

    (a) May be requested anonymously

    (b) The Training Information Resources coordinator notifies the commander, and the commander determines if Training Information Resources are appropriate to address the issue.

5. <u>COMMANDER'S RESPONSIBILITIES UNDER THE IRS</u>

   a. Set the example.

   b. Establish a command climate that allows and encourages individuals to resolve conflicts between themselves without fear of reprisal.

   c. Keep an open mind. Listen and do not filter.

   d. Do not ignore the behavior.

   e. Know when to get involved and when not to (if IRS is working, give it a chance to resolve the conflict).

(1) Determine if the IRS has been used; if not, encourage its use if appropriate.

(2) Do not intervene when conflict is being resolved by those involved.

(3) Intervene when necessary. Get involved when:

    (a) You are approached by recipient, offending person, or another person;

    (b) You observe inappropriate behavior; or

    (c) You are otherwise made aware of a situation which cannot be resolved.

(4) Take or support actions to reach resolutions. Provide resource materials as appropriate.

(5) In any case, follow up and provide feedback to the individuals involved.

(6) Report/take action on all criminal red zone behavior, inform the appropriate authorities.

(7) Avoid further traumatizing recipient; e.g., if you need to physically separate personnel, whenever feasible move the offending person, not the recipient.

(8) Make referrals to support services as warranted.

6. <u>IRS IS SUPPORTED BY TWO ELEMENTS</u> (available through the EOAs)

    a. <u>"Resolving Conflict" Pamphlet</u>

       (1) Stand alone "How to" guide

       (2) Resource to augment IRS lesson plan

       (3) Introduces IRS elements

       (4) Empowers reader to implement system to resolve conflict at lowest possible level.

    b. <u>Training Information Resources Library</u>. Located at major installations, managed by EOAs.

APPENDIX F

DEFINITIONS

To ensure uniform understanding of the terms that have special significance and/or meaning relative to the Marine Corps Equal Opportunity Program (EOP), the following definitions are provided. (Terms that have special meaning relative to specific chapters of this Manual are defined in those chapters.)

1. <u>Anti-Semitism</u>. Hostility toward or discrimination against Jews as a religious or racial group.

2. <u>Beliefs</u>. Judgments or expectancies which one may hold.

3. <u>Bias</u>. A mental leaning or inclination; partiality; prejudice.

4. <u>Category</u>. A specifically defined division in a system of classification.

5. <u>Chain of Command</u>. The succession of commanding officers from a superior to a subordinate through which command is exercised.

6. <u>Complaint</u>. An allegation of unlawful discrimination based on age, color, national origin, race, ethnic group, religion or gender.

   <u>Informal Complaint</u>. Allegation of unlawful discrimination or sexual harassment, made either orally or in writing, that is resolved utilizing the informal resolution system.

   <u>Formal Complaint</u>. Allegation of unlawful discrimination or sexual harassment that is submitted via Request Mast, charge sheet, congressional inquiry, DON or IGMC complaint line, Article 138 of the UCMJ, Article 1150 of the Navy Regulations, or initiation of administrative or criminal investigation.

7. <u>Complainant</u>. A person who submits allegations of unlawful discrimination or sexual harassment.

8. <u>Condition</u>. To make some aspect of another's employment, career, pay, duty assignment, benefits, or privileges contingent upon fulfillment of some requirement the maker thereof has no right to impose.

9. <u>Culture</u>. The learned and shared behaviors and perceptions of a group which have been transmitted from generation to generation through a shared symbol system.

10. <u>Cultural Diversity</u>. A condition in a group of people or organization brought about by the gender, religion, racial, cultural, and social differences that the individuals naturally bring to the group or organization.

11. <u>Discrimination</u>. The act, policy, or procedure that arbitrarily denies equal opportunity because of age, color, national origin, race, ethnic group, religion or gender to an individual or group of individuals.

12. <u>Disparaging Terms</u>. Terms used to degrade or imply negative connotations pertaining to age, color, national origin, race, ethnic group, religion or

gender. Such terms include insults, printed material, visual material, signs, symbols, posters, or insignia.

13. Equal Opportunity (EO). The right of all persons to participate in, and benefit from, programs and activities for which they are qualified. These programs and activities will be free from social, personal, or institutional barriers that prevent people from rising to the highest level of responsibility possible. Persons will be evaluated on individual merit, fitness, and capability, regardless of age, color, national origin, race, ethnic group, religion or gender.

14. Equal Opportunity Advisor (EOA). These Marines are assigned to major Marine installations and their mission is to provide information, assistance, and advice on all EO matters to installation and tenant commanders (MCO 5354.3).

15. Equal Opportunity Climate. An atmosphere in which all individuals are treated equitably without regard to age, color, national origin, race, ethnic group, religion or gender.

16. Equal Opportunity in Off-Base Housing. The portion of the Marine Corps EOP that supports the Department of Defense's and the Marine Corps' goal to eliminate discrimination against military and DoD civilian personnel in off-base housing.

17. Equal Employment Opportunity Program. The comprehensive program through which the Marine Corps implements its policy to provide equal opportunity in employment for all qualified civilian personnel (MCO 12713.6).

18. Ethnicity. That which sets off a group by race (defined as genetic), religion (preferred denomination), national origin (country of one's ancestors), or some combination of these categories.

19. Ethnic Group. A segment of the population that possesses common characteristics and cultural heritage.

20. Ethnic and Racial Categories. Basic ethnic and racial categories for DoD reporting are defined as follows:

    a. American Indian or Alaska Native. A person having origins in the original peoples of North and South America (including Central America), and who maintains tribal affiliation and/or community attachment.

    b. Asian. A person having origins in any of the original peoples of the Far East, Southeast Asia, Indian subcontinent. This area includes Cambodia, China, India, Japan, Korea, Malaysia, Pakistan, Philippine Islands, Thailand and Vietnam.

    c. Black or African American. A person having origins in any of the original peoples of Africa.

    d. Hispanic or Latino. A person having origins in any of the original peoples of Mexico, Puerto Rico, Cuba, Central or South America, or of other Spanish culture or origin, regardless of race.

    e. Native Hawaiian or Other Pacific Islander. A person having origins in any of the original peoples of Hawaii, Guam, Samoa, or other Pacific Islands.

    f. White. A person having origins in any of the original peoples of Europe, North Africa, or the Middle East.

21. Hostile Environment. A type of harassment that occurs when unwelcome behavior of one or more persons in a workplace produces a work atmosphere which is offensive, intimidating, or abusive to another person using the reasonable person standard.

22. Human Relations. The social relations between human beings; a course, study, or program designed to develop better interpersonal and intergroup adjustments.

23. Informal Resolution System (IRS). A process that uses the common sense approach for resolving conflict at the lowest possible level.

24. Institutional Discrimination. Policies, procedures, and practices that, intentionally or unintentionally, lead to differential treatment of selected identifiable groups and which, through usage and custom, have attained official or semiofficial acceptance in the routine functioning of the organization/institution.

25. Legal Sufficiency Review. The review of an investigation into a formal complaint of unlawful discrimination or sexual harassment to determine whether:

    a. The investigation complies with all applicable legal and administrative requirements,

    b. The investigation adequately addresses the matters complained of,

    c. The evidence supports the findings of the investigating officer or board,

    d. The conclusions and recommendations of the investigating officer or board are consistent with the findings, and,

    e. Any errors or irregularities exist, and, if so, their legal effect, if any.

26. Minority. A group which differs from the predominant section of a larger group in one or more characteristics; e.g., ethnic background, language, culture, or religion and, as a result, is often subjected to differential treatment. Race and ethnic codes of minorities are published in MCO P1080.20 (MCTFSCODESMAN).

27. Objective. Defines the basic result desired.

28. Prejudice. An attitude, judgment or opinion, without regard to pertinent fact, that is typically expressed in suspicion, fear, hostility, or intolerance of certain people, customs, and ideas.

29. Proposed Corrective Action. Plan of action developed to resolve identified areas of concern.

30. <u>Protected Communication</u>. Lawful communication to a member of Congress, an IG, or to any other person or organization (including any person or organization in the chain of command) designated to receive such communications, to which a person makes a complaint or discloses information that he or she reasonably believes evidences a violation of law or regulation (including those covering unlawful discrimination and sexual harassment).

31. <u>"Quid Pro Quo" or "This for That"</u>. A type of sexual harassment that occurs when submitting to or rejecting such behavior is used as a basis for decisions affecting any person's job, pay, or career. This could be a promise of employment, a promotion, a threat of or an actual demotion, a duty assignment, or a positive or negative performance evaluation.

32. <u>Race</u>. A division of human beings identified by the possession of traits that are transmissible by descent and that are sufficient to characterize persons possessing these traits as a distinctive human genotype.

33. <u>Race/Ethnic Groups</u>. The race/ethnic groups for Marine Corps reporting are the same as listed under Ethnic and Racial Categories.

34. <u>Racial/Ethnic Incident</u>. An incident that involves members of two or more racial/ethnic groups, and racial/ethnic factors were the precipitating cause, or it became a motivating factor. If an incident involves members of only one racial/ethnic origin but is directed at another racial/ethnic group, it should be considered a racial/ethnic incident.

35. <u>Racism</u>. A belief or attitude that race determines an individual's traits and capabilities and that racial differences produce a natural superiority of a particular race. Behavior or conditions that foster stereotypes of social roles based on race.

36. <u>Reasonable Person Standard</u>. An objective test used to determine if behavior constitutes sexual harassment. This standard considers what a reasonable person's reaction would have been under similar circumstances and in a similar environment. The reasonable person standard considers the recipient's perspective and not stereotyped notions of acceptable behavior. For example, a work environment in which sexual slurs, the display of sexually suggestive calendars, or other offensive sexual behavior abound can constitute sexual harassment even if other people might deem it to be harmless or insignificant.

37. <u>Recipient</u>. Any person subjected to harassment or discrimination (also referred to as complainant).

38. <u>Reprisal</u>. Taking or threatening to take an unfavorable personnel action, or withholding or threatening to withhold a favorable personnel action, or any other act of retaliation, against a military member for making or preparing a protected communication.

39. <u>Request Mast</u>. The principal means for a Marine to formally communicate a grievance to, or seek assistance, from his or her commander.

40. <u>Sexism</u>. Behavior, conditions or attitudes that foster stereotypes of roles, prejudice or discrimination based on the sex of an individual.

41. Sexual Harassment (DON Definition, SECNAVINST 5300.26B)

a. Sexual harassment is a form of discrimination that involves unwelcome sexual advances, requests for sexual favors, and other verbal or physical conduct of a sexual nature when:

(1) Submission to such conduct is made either explicitly or implicitly a term or condition of a person's job, pay, career, or,

(2) Submission to or rejection of such conduct by a person is used as a basis for career, or employment decisions affecting that person, or,

(3) Such conduct has the purpose or effect of unreasonably interfering with an individual's work performance or creates an intimidating, hostile, or offensive working environment.

b. The above definition emphasizes that workplace conduct, to be actionable as "abusive work environment" harassment, need not result in concrete psychological harm to the victim, but rather need only be so severe or pervasive that a reasonable person would perceive, and the victim does perceive, the work environment as hostile or abusive [Note: "workplace" is an expansive term for military members and may include conduct on or off duty, 24 hours a day.]

c. Any person in a supervisory or command position who uses or condones implicit or explicit sexual behavior to control, influence, or affect the career, pay, or job of a military member or civilian employee is engaging in sexual harassment. Similarly, any military member or civilian employee who makes deliberate or repeated unwelcome verbal comments, gestures, or physical contact of a sexual nature in the workplace is also engaging in sexual harassment.

42. Training and Information Resources (TIR) Library. A library of various books, videos, and lesson plans on equal opportunity issues located with the installation EOA's office.

43. Unwelcome. Conduct that is not solicited and which is considered objectionable by the person to whom it is directed and which is found to be undesirable or offensive using a reasonable person standard.

44. Values. Those things, people, and ideas that are important to an individual.

45. Work Environment. The workplace or any other place that is work-connected, as well as the conditions or atmosphere under which people are required to work.

APPENDIX G

LIST OF APPLICABLE/HELPFUL REFERENCES

1. DoDDir 1350.25, The Department of Defense Military Equal Opportunity Program

2. DoDINST 1350.3, Affirmative Action Planning and Assessment Process

3. DoDDir 5500.7, Standards of Conduct, and DoDDir 5500.7-R, Joint Ethics Regulation (JER)

4. DoDDir 7050.6, Military Whistleblower Protection

5. SECNAVINST 1600.1, Relationships with Organizations Which Seek to Represent or Organize Members of the Armed Forces in Negotiation or Collective Bargaining

6. SECNAVINST 1920.6, Administrative Separation of Officers

7. SECNAVINST 5211.5, Department of the Navy Privacy Act (PA) Program

8. SECNAVINST 5300.26, Department of the Navy (DON) Policy on Sexual Harassment

9. SECNAVINST 5370.7, Military Whistleblower Protection

10. SECNAVINST 5370.8, Military Reprisal Investigations

11. SECNAVINST 5520.3, Criminal and Security Investigations and Related Activities Within the Department of the Navy

12. SECNAVINST 5800.11, Victim and Witness Assistance Program

13. SECNAVINST 12720.5, The Department of the Navy Civilian Equal Employment Opportunity Program (enclosing DoDDir 1440.1, The DoD Civilian Equal Employment Opportunity (EEO) Program).

14. MCO 1000.9, Sexual Harassment

15. MCO 1620.2 Armed Forces Disciplinary Control Board and Off-Installation Military Enforcement Services

16. MCO 1700.23, Request Mast

17. MCO P5354.1, Marine Corps Equal Opportunity Manual

18. MCO 5354.3, Equal Opportunity Advisors

19. MCO 5730.4, Dissident Protest Activity

20. MCO 5740.2 w/Erratum, OPREP-3 SIR: Serious Incident Reports

21. MCO 12713.6, Equal Employment Opportunity Program

22. JAGINST 5800.7, Manual of the Judge Advocate General (JAGMAN)

23. Manual for Courts-Martial

24. U. S. Navy Regulations, Articles 1150 (Complaint of Wrongdoing), 1165 (Fraternization) and 1166 (Sexual Harassment) {OPNAVINST 3120.32}

25. OCPMINST 12713.2A, Department of the Navy Discrimination Complaints (CPI 713)

26. Team Marine Lesson Plan, PCN 50100379300, Core Values VHS Tape, PCN 50100379400.

27. Processing EO/EEO Complaints - A Commander's Handbook, PCN 50100379600

28. Informal Resolution System (IRS), PCN 50100379700

29. NAVPERS 15620, Resolving Conflict, PCN 20606795000

30. User's Guide to Marine Corps Leadership Training (NAVMC 2767)

APPENDIX H

INSPECTOR GENERAL CHECKLIST

1. Has the commander established policies and procedures to ensure the periodic assessment and update of his/her equal opportunity program, to include making equal opportunity and sexual harassment a special interest item in the command's inspection program?

2. Does the Equal Opportunity Advisor serve in the billet to which assigned and provide instructions, assistance and advice to commander(s) on equal opportunity matters and climate?

3. Has the command published and displayed their equal opportunity policy statement and does it include sexual harassment and the possible consequences for engaging in discrimination and sexual harassment?

4. Has the command published procedures for receiving discrimination and sexual harassment complaints, and established procedures to ensure they are thoroughly investigated and resolved within the timelines, without reprisal or retaliation?

5. Has the command designated, in writing, an Equal Opportunity Representative who assists in the commander establishing equal opportunity policies?

6. Does the command complete and maintain copies of all required annual reports?

7. Does the command review statistical data related to personnel actions for possible discriminatory practices?

8. Does the commander ensure that conscientious efforts are made to provide the media with news and articles featuring the accomplishments of all Marines?

9. Does the command conduct all required equal opportunity training?

10. Is equal opportunity included in leadership training?

11. Are all formal allegations of discrimination and sexual harassment properly reported?

12. Is immediate and effective action taken to eliminate discrimination when identified?

13. Are legal sufficiency and equal opportunity reviews conducted on all discrimination and sexual harassment investigations?

14. Has the command conducted an equal opportunity survey within 90 day of the commander's assignment?

APPENDIX I

EO INVESTIGATION REVIEW CRITERIA

1. Date of review:

2. Service: Marine Corps

3. Location of files:

4. Complainant name/case number/identifier:

5. Date complaint filed:

6. Date investigation initiated:

7. Date investigation completed:

8. Type/authority for investigation:

9. Complaint factors:

    a. Same chain of command? Different chain of command?

    b. Conduct occurred on/off base? On/off duty?

    c. Type of EO complaint: race, color, religion, gender, national origin age, sexual harassment, ethnicity and color.

    d. Nature of allegations: gestures, verbal, physical, personnel action, other.

    e. Allegations were: substantiated, partially substantiated, unsubstantiated.

10. Complainant demographics: rank, gender, ethnic origin, age, race

11. Alleged Offender demographics: rank, gender, ethnic origin, age, race

12. Investigating/Inquiry Officer demographics: rank, gender, ethnic origin, age, race

13. Investigating/Inquiry Officer (IO) factors:

    a. Who conducted investigation - commander, assigned investigating officer, EO Advisor, Inspector General?

    b. Did the appointment of the IO comply with governing regulations? What process was used to select the IO?

    c. Was the IO outside the rating chain of command of the parties to the complaint?

    d. Was the IO previously experienced in conducting investigations?

e. What training/guidance, if any, was provided to the IO? Did it include legal advice? Technical advice from DEOMI trained EO specialist? other EO Advisor? Explain.

f. Did the IO have or obtain a working knowledge of DoD/Service EO policy prior to conducting the investigation?

14. Investigation Factors:

a. Were all allegations thoroughly addressed? If not, explain.

b. Is there any relevant information the complainant submitted the IO did not include or address?

c. Did the investigating agency/IO define the issues subject to investigation? If so, were they properly defined so as not to limit the full scope of the complaint?

d. Was the complainant interviewed at the beginning of the investigation?

e. Was the complainant kept informed of the status of the complaint/investigation?

f. Was the alleged offender interviewed?

g. Were witnesses listed by the complainant interviewed?

h. Were witnesses listed by the alleged offender interviewed?

i. Were any key witnesses not interviewed? Explain.

j. Is there documentation of witnesses' testimony, i.e., summarized, taped, verbatim, statement?

k. Were witnesses given the opportunity to sign or otherwise validate their summarized testimony as an accurate representation of what they said?

l. Was the testimony taken under oath?

m. Does the investigation include a thorough review of the circumstance under which the alleged discrimination occurred?

n. Did the investigation include an analysis of how the victim was treated compared to others within the complainant's demographic group and with those of other demographic groups?

o. Did the investigation identify any related policies or practices or issues that may constitute, or appear to constitute, discrimination even though they may not have been raised by the complainant?

p. If discrimination and/or the allegations were unsubstantiated, were any management deficiencies identified that may have contributed to the allegations addressed and corrected?

q. Is there documentation of the IO's questions? If so, were the questions worded in such a manner to specifically address the allegations? If there is no documentation of the questions, do the responses specifically address the allegations?

r. Did the IO clearly and objectively present the facts of the case?

s. Are the opinions of the IO clearly identified as such and distinct from the factual and documentary evidence?

t. Is there any evidence of bias (a highly personal and unreasoned distortion of judgment) by the IO?

u. Is there any evidence the complainant rather than the complaint was investigated?

v. Are the conclusions sound, logical and supported by the facts?

w. Are the recommendations, if present, appropriate for the circumstances?

x. Was there a legal sufficiency review of the report? If so, was report found legally sufficient?

y. Was an EO functional review of the report conducted at any level for adherence to EO policy and definitions? If so, was the review by a DEOMI-trained EO Advisor?

z. Did the findings and the report conform to EO policy and definitions? Explain.

aa. Were there deficiencies, discrepancies, incongruities or nonconcurrences in the findings, conclusions or recommendations? Were they noted and corrected? Explain.

ab. Is there any evidence that the conclusions were based on an erroneous interpretation of law or regulation or misapplication of established policy, or constitute a precedent involving new or not yet reviewed policy consideration that may have effects beyond the actual case at hand?

ac. Were essential documents relevant to a fair determination of the underlying allegations contained in the file?

15. Corrective action:

a. What corrective action, if any, was taken?

b. Is corrective action documented in the case file?

c. Was there any follow-up regarding the effectiveness of the corrective action taken?

16. Responses to complainants/subjects:

a. Was a response provided to the complainant?

b. Was response written or verbal?

    c. Was feedback documented in the case file?

    d. Did the response adequately address the complainant's allegations?

    e. Was verbal or written advice given to the complainant to report any reprisal taken against them for filing EO complaint?

    f. Was the subject and alleged offender advised of the outcome?

17. <u>Appeal and redress options</u>:

    a. Was the complainant advised of appeal and/or redress options?

    b. Did the complainant seek appeal or redress of the outcome of the complaint?

    c. Did the complainant present new and material evidence not readily available during the investigation?

    d. Did any appeal or redress authority find an erroneous interpretation of law or regulation or misapplication of established policy, or that the conclusions were of a precedent involving new or not yet reviewed policy consideration that may have effects beyond the actual case at hand?

    e. Did the appeal or redress authority adequately and appropriately consider the complainant's request for further reviews?

APPENDIX J

LIST OF SPECIAL EMPHASIS OBSERVANCES

The special emphasis observances listed here are established and commemorated throughout DoD. From time to time, Congress and the President may establish other occasions that may require action. Commanders are expected to publicize these events, establish policy that supports and allows personnel to have a reasonable opportunity to participate in these events.

Month: January
Dates: Third Monday
Observance: Martin Luther King, Jr., Birthday
Authority/comment: Public Law 98-144, Nov 83 (Federal Holiday)

Month: February
Dates: 1-28/29
Observance: African American History Month
Authority/comment: First Presidential Proclamation, Feb 76

Month: March
Dates: 1-31
Observance: Women's History Month
Authority/comment: Public Law 100-0, Mar 87

Month: April/May
Dates: Sunday to Sunday for Week Incorporating Yom Hashoah
Observance: "Days of Remembrance" for Victims of the Holocaust
Authority/comment: Public Law 96-388, Oct 80

Month: May
Dates: 1-31
Observance: Asian Pacific American Heritage Month
Authority/comment: First Presidential Proclamation, May 91

Month: August
Dates: 26
Observance: Women's Equality Day
Authority/comment: First Presidential Proclamation, Aug 73

Month: September/October
Dates: 15 Sep - 15 Oct
Observance: National Hispanic Heritage Month
Authority/comment: Public Law 100-402, Aug 88

Month: November
Dates: 1-30
Observance: National Native American Indian Heritage Month
Authority/comment: Public Law 102-188, Mar 92

APPENDIX K

DEOMI MOBILE TRAINING TEAM (MTT) REQUEST

From: Commanding General/Officer making request
To: Commandant, Defense Equal Opportunity Management Institute,
        Code DL (MTT), Patrick AFB, Florida 32925-3399

Subj: REQUEST FOR MOBILE TRAINING TEAM (MTT) VISIT

1. Request DEOMI provide MTT for the purpose of presenting the (enter
type of EO training requested, e.g., 2-day Senior Leadership Equal
Opportunity Training to Commanding Officers and their Sergeants Major
and First Sergeants) at (Name of Command).

2. Point of contact is _____.

                              Signature of requesting commander

Copy to:
CMC (MPE)

APPENDIX L

REQUEST FORM FOR DEOMI MILITARY EQUAL OPPORTUNITY CLIMATE SURVEY (MEOCS)

MEOCS REQUEST FORM (PLEASE TYPE)

NOTES: - We will provide enough answer sheets to complete the MEOCS; however, we only provide one copy of the survey booklet It is the organization's responsibility to reproduce the survey booklets required
- For organizations with more than 100 personnel: Please aim for a response rate of at least 50% of the organization's total strength
- When using versions other than the SUEOCS we need at least 50 responses in order to process your survey
- For organizations with less than 50 personnel: unless we have advised otherwise, please mark the Small Unit Survey Block in part 13 below Also, we need at least 7 responses to process a SUEOCS

1 Grade of requesting commander/organizational head (O-3, O-6, GS-11, SES-4, etc): _____

2 Number of people intended to survey: _____

3 Organization's present location -- State, Country, Area -- (EXAMPLES -- KENTUCKY, JAPAN, GERMANY, PACIFIC): _____

4a Branch of service (CIRCLE ONE):   USAF   USA   USCG   USMC   USN   DoD/Joint Service   Federal Civilian   Other: _____

4b Service Component (CIRCLE ONE):   Active Duty   Reserve   National Guard   Other:__(active _____

5 You will administer MEOCS to (CIRCLE ONE): Military Only   Civilian Only   Both Military & Civilian

6 Organization's major command -- MACOM, MAJCOM (EXAMPLES -- TRADOC, CG DISTRICT 2, PACFLEET, AMC): _____

7 Organization's Unit Identification Code (UIC) (PAS code for USAF): _____

8 Organization's mission (CIRCLE ONE):   Combat   Combat Support   Other Support

9 Commander's title, Organization's name and Official address: _____
(EXAMPLE -- See Our Mailing Address Below -- Item #15)   _____
_____   _____

10 Survey administrator -- Rank and Name: _____ DSN Phone Number:_____

          E-Mail Address _____ Commercial Phone Number _____

11 Has the organization taken MEOCS before?   No   Yes   Date or Dates: _____

12 Demographics of personnel as identified in #2 above:

	MALE			FEMALE		
	OFFICER	ENLISTED	CIVILIAN	OFFICER	ENLISTED	CIVILIAN
MAJORITY						
MINORITY						
TOTALS						

"MINORITY" Includes the following racial/ethnic groups: Black/African-American, Hispanic, Asian-American/Pacific Islander, & Native-American/Alaskan-Native. "MAJORITY" Includes those not in the groups listed above.

13 Please indicate which version of MEOCS you would like to request; short descriptions of each can be found on the reverse side of this form:

Standard MEOCS (2.3)		MEOCS-LITE		Small Unit (SUEOCS)	
Std. MEOCS Male Only (2.3 M)		MEOCS-EEO			

14 Commander's/Organizational Head's signature: Signature: _____

   NOTE: The requesting commander   Rank & Name:_____
   must sign the request

15 Forward by either mail or fax: Commandant   E-Mail POC at DEOMI: ian dames@patrick af mil
                    DEOMI/DR (MEOCS)   DEOMI Internet address: https://www patrick af mil/deomi/deomi htm
                    740 O'Malley Road, MS 9121
                    Patrick AFB, FL 32925-3399

          Our phone number is: DSN 854-2675 or Commercial (321) 494-2675.
          Our FAX number is: DSN 854-4116 or Commercial (321) 494-4116.

Revised 23 July 2002		FOR DEOMI USE ONLY				
ADMIN NUMBER	REC'D REQUEST DATE	SENT SURVEYS DATE	REC'D COMPLETED FORMS DATE	SENT FINAL RPT DATE	NUMBER OF FORMS REQUESTED	NUMBER OF FORMS SENT
SITE NUMBER :	#FORMSRECEIVED	MISC INFO:				

APPENDIX M

REQUEST MAST FORM (FRONT SIDE)

MCO 1700.23E

MARINE CORPS REQUEST MAST APPLICATION
NAVMC 11296 (Rev. 6-97)
SN: 0000-00-888-0350   U/I: EA

PRIVACY ACT STATEMENT

Authority: Title 5, U. S. Code 301; Title 10, USC Section 5013

Priincipal Purpose: Formal filing of complaints/problems to command personnel.

Routine Uses: To provide a record to facilitate personnel management actions and decisions; to serve as a date source for complaint/problem information and resolution efforts.
Disclosure: Disclosure is voluntary. Failure to complete the requested items could result in delayed command action and/or an inaccurate/incomplete analysis of the complaint/problem.

PART I TO BE COMPLETED BY THE APPLICANT		
1. NAME:	2. RANK:	3. SSN:
4. UNIT:	5. RACE/ETHNIC GROUP:	
6. GENDER:	7. DATE:	

8a. I desire to Request Mast with: (Provide the name and billet of the Commanding Officer with whom you desire to communicate.):

8b. NATURE OF COMPLAINT/PROBLEM: (Give in as much detail as possible the basis of your complaint; describe the incident(s)/behavior(s) and date(s) of the occurrence(s); the names of the individuals involved, witnesses and to whom it may have been previously reported. Include any other information relevant to your compliant/problem. Attach additional sheets, as needed).

8c. REQUESTED REMEDY/OUTCOME. (Clearly state what assistance or complaint resolution you are seeking from the commanding officer named in 0a above.)

9. AFFDAVIT

I, _____ , have read this statement which begins in Block 8b on this page (page 1) and ends on page _____ . I fully understand the statement made by me and certify the statement is true. I have initialed all corrections. I make this formal statement without threat of punishment and without coercion, unlawful influence, or unlawful inducement.

_____
(SIGNATURE OF APPLICANT/DATE)

A-1   Appendix A to ENCLOSURE (2)

MARINE CORPS EQUAL OPPORTUNITY MANUAL

REQUEST MAST FORM (REVERSE SIDE)

MCO 1700.23E

NAVMC 11296 (Rev 6-97) PAGE 2

PART II: TO BE COMPLETED BY THE OFFICER CONDUCTING REQUEST MAST

10. DISPOSITION: (Provide a detailed explanation of actions taken or attempted to resolve the complaint/problem, to include any other referrals. If an inquiry/investigation was initiated as a result of this complaint, provide the type conducted and the results. Attach additional sheets as necessary.)

COMMANDING OFFICER SIGNATURE/DATE

PART III APPLICANT'S ACKNOWLEDGMENT OF REQUEST MAST

(Applicant should initial/complete the appropriate statement(s))

_____ I have had the opportunity to communicate directly with my Commanding Officer named in Block 8a and understand the disposition or probable disposition of my problem/complaint.

_____ I have had the opportunity to communicate directly with_____
(name and billet of commanding officer subordinate to officer named in Block 8a), understand the disposition or probable disposition of my problem/complaint, and voluntarily withdraw this Request Mast.

_____ I have not had the opportunity to communicate directly with my Commanding Officer named in Block 8a.

_____ I have had the opportunity to communicate directly with my Commanding Officer named in Block 8a but have not been informed of the disposition or probable disposition of my problem/complaint.

WITNESS' SIGNATURE/DATE   APPLICANT'S SIGNATURE/DATE

Appendix A to ENCLOSURE (2)   **A-2**

M-2

APPENDIX N

RESOURCES AVAILABLE

1. <u>NEWSLETTER</u>. Three times a year the CMC (MPE) will publish a newsletter (Equal Opportunity Newsline). This newsletter is available on the HQMC EO Website. It provides information and updates concerning EO issues.

2. <u>DEOMI COURSES</u>. Frequently, the CMC (MPE) will announce class schedules available from DEOMI. Normally, these courses are ideal for officers as well as senior SNCO's in leadership positions (SgtMaj/1stSgt). The following courses are available through DEOMI:

<u>Equal Opportunity Advisor Reserve Components Course (EOARCC)</u>
<u>Length</u>: Phase I: (Distance Learning/Correspondence Course) Student has 3 to 6 months to complete Phase I studies, Phase II: 3 weeks of resident training.
<u>Target Audience</u>: Reservists and civilians who advise reserve component Commanders on EO matters.
<u>Method of Instruction</u>: Distance Learning (DL)/correspondence, small group discussions/exercises, and lectures
<u>Course Description</u>: The Reserve Components Course is equivalent to the EOA Course. Upon enrollment in the resident course, students are mailed a packet of training materials to complete Phase I. Phase I consists of a two part nonresident course of study that focuses on Interpersonal Awareness, and Ethnic Studies and is accomplished through distance learning/correspondence. After completing a multiple choice/true/false test with 70% accuracy during Phase I, students are eligible to complete Phase II. Phase II is 3 weeks of resident training that focuses on small group activities conducted to enhance the DL portion and the Dynamics of Power. Phase II also includes 4 days of Service Specific Training. Graduates are qualified to serve as EOAs in Reserve and National Guard Units.

<u>Equal Opportunity Program Managers Course (EOPMC)</u>
<u>Length</u>: 6 Weeks
<u>Target Audience</u>: Military and civilian personnel who manage EO programs and supervise EOAs
<u>Method of Instruction</u>: Interactive lectures, large and small group discussions, experiential exercises, feedback, group dynamics and development, and guest lectures.
<u>Course Description</u>: The course develops a base of knowledge and skills that prepare graduates to effectively manage the EO program and to provide advice and assistance to EOAs. Studies focus on the inter/intrapersonal and organizational aspects of EO. Studies progress from communication to individual and group behavior. The course entails a 3-week core portion and a 3-week Service Specific portion. The attendees are integrated into the Service Specific portion of DEOMI's EOA course. Instructional methodologies include: student-centered lectures, small group processing, role playing, student exercises and presentations, debate, reactive cultural paper, and guest speakers.

<u>Equal Opportunity Orientation Workshop (EOOW)</u>
<u>Length</u>: 5 Days
<u>Target Audience</u>: This workshop is designed for officers (O4 and above) and civilians including legal officers, chaplains, and inspector general personnel in leadership positions. Highly recommended for officers (O4 and above) about to take command responsibilities. This workshop is not a substitute for EOA or EOPMC.

Method of Instruction: Seminar, small group discussion, and practical exercises
Course Description: The goal of the workshop is to impart upon the participants the manner in which EO issues impact unit cohesion, mission accomplishment, combat readiness and increased awareness, sensitivity, and understanding of EO issues. The workshop incorporates participants' personal and professional experiences. Participants are encouraged to bring real-world issues and problems to the table, give and receive feedback, understand the impact of their behavior on others, group and on larger organizational systems. The Workshop also provides attendees the opportunity to benefit from student and organizational diversity of working issues.

Senior Enlisted EO Workshop (SEEOW)
Length: 5 Days
Target Audience: Master Sergeants, First Sergeants, Master Gunnery Sergeants, Sergeants Major
Method of Instruction: Seminar
Course Description: The goal of the workshop is to impart upon the participants the manner in which EO issues impact unit cohesion, mission accomplishment, combat readiness and increased awareness, sensitivity, and understanding of EO issues. The program is divided into the following topic areas:

        Socialization and Values
        Dynamics of Power
        Sexism and Sexual Harassment
        Leading a Culturally Diverse Work Force
        Contemporary (Emerging) EO Issues
        Future Focus

The training methodology is interactive lectures, video presentations followed by discussions, case study and scenario solving, and facilitated action planning. Facilitators are experienced subject-matter experts and are graduates of DEOMI's Resident EOA Course

Mediation Course
Length: 1 Week
Target Audience: Military and civilian personnel who have attended previous DEOMI Civilian EEO or Military Equal Opportunity Advisors Courses who need to learn how to mediate disputes concerning personnel or Equal Opportunity (EO)/Equal Employment Opportunity (EEO) issues in the Department of Defense.
Method of Instruction: Practical exercises and lectures
Course Description: This course builds on knowledge and skills developed in previous DEOMI Civilian EEO or Military Equal Opportunity Advisor Courses. It provides participants with skills necessary to mediate disputes at their commands, installations, and activities. Graduates are certified to mediate civilian personnel and equal opportunity disputes within DoD.

To register, contact CMC (MPE) at DSN 278-9371 or Commercial (703) 784-9371 and ask for the Senior EOA.

3. Publications Available. The following publications are available through MCLB, Albany, GA:

Publications	PCN
Team Marine	50100379300
Processing EO/EEO Complaints - A Commander's Handbook	50100379600
Informal Resolution System (IRS) Lesson Plan	50100379700
Resolving Conflicts Pamphlets (IRS)	20600795000

www.ingramcontent.com/pod-product-compliance
Lightning Source LLC
Chambersburg PA
CBHW081132290526
45795CB00006B/2206